Family Therapy

An Interactional Approach

Family Therapy
An Interactional Approach

Maurizio Andolfi
Italian Society for Family Therapy
Rome, Italy

Translated by
Helene Raff Cassin

With a Foreword by
Carl A. Whitaker

Plenum Press · New York and London

Library of Congress Cataloging in Publication Data

Andolfi, Maurizio.
  Family therapy.

  Translation of La terapia con la famiglia.
  Bibliography: p.
  Includes index.
  1. Family psychotherapy. I. Title.
  [DNLM: 1. Family therapy. WM430.5.F2 A552f]
  RC488.5.A513   616.8'915   78-27741
  ISBN 0-306-40200-9

First Printing — June 1979
Second Printing — December 1980

This translation has been published with the permission of
Casa Editrice Astrolabio-Ubaldini Editore, the publisher of
the original Italian edition, which was published in Rome in
1977 under the title *La Terapia con la Famiglia.*

© 1979 Plenum Press, New York
A Division of Plenum Publishing Corporation
227 West 17th Street, New York, N.Y. 10011

Printed in the United States of America

To the memory of my brother Silvano

Prendere il mondo a braccetto
carezzarlo dolcemente.
Che follia.
Così ho detto a uno specchio
che mai riproduce
la mia immagine vera.
Arrossendo in viso
ha allargato le braccia
l'uomo nello specchio.
An umbrella maker
vende i suoi ombrelli
sognando la pioggia
che bagna la terra
per avere un buon pane.
—Speriamo che piova
domani
a Dublino—
ho detto allo specchio:
e lui sorrideva
di un mio vero sorriso.

Go arm in arm with the world.
Caress it gently.
What folly!
I said to a mirror
which never reflects
my true image.
Blushing,
he opened his arms wide,
the man in the mirror.
An umbrella maker
sells his umbrellas
dreaming of the rain
which soaks into the earth
to give him good bread.
—Let's hope it rains
in Dublin
tomorrow—
I said into the mirror,
and he smiled
with my true smile.

—SILVANO ANDOLFI

Foreword

Dr. Maurizio Andolfi, "Andi" to my dog and me, is one of the fourth-generation family therapy theorists. This book, which he calls "interactional," is probably one you would not enjoy. Maybe you could give it to a rival colleague on his birthday. Combining the teachings of Zwerling and Laperriere with Ferber is confusing. Add to that a Horney analysis and stir with two ounces of Minuchin and a dram of Haley, and Andolfi becomes distracting to his friends and colleagues. His work with Cancrini reacculturated him somewhat, but a Roman is a Roman, and, of course, he could not understand such problems as those we conquer in the United States.

Assuming your rival is a well-trained, cause-and-effect thinker, you might find ways to watch him squirm. If he has not tried paradoxical methods, expect him to take a long vacation from work. If he is already a good family therapist, he may become a bit hypomanic, and his team may talk to you in private. Encourage them to suggest that he work harder and stop reading the book or, better still, donate it to the social-work school library; they will read anything. If the team complains that the book advises teaching sick families how to be their own therapists, resist any impulse to check this out. No family could become self-reparative when it is already dysfunctional. We know that professional help is the only hope. We also know that the therapist must not interact with the family. If they complain that the team director is laughing up a storm or retching at meals, reassure them that he is just being loosened up inside by absurd triangle talk and stories about family stress patterns that Andi probably read in an "Antichrist" textbook. Do not show any response if they talk about teaching mothers and children to play during the interview, while Andi whispers to the father in the next room. It is just a fairy story. If they infer that their training system is changing and that sculpting, creative tasks, and silly rules make work enjoyable, be certain to warn them that science can correct all this in time, but that reading further could upset long years of experience and make new experiences swing their doors till the rusty hinges squeak.

Furthermore, if your esteemed rival accosts you himself about the three kinds of therapeutic tasks and the classification of family rules, suggest—gently, of course—that he forget them and also should not read any stories of a therapist and one family member colluding behind the family's back. Helping a well family member who is playing sick is absurd and counterproductive at the very least.

If your rival quotes Andi as saying that a paradox is a situation in which an affirmation is true if, and only if, it is false, please insist that such nonsense is merely an Italian jest about our high-quality theories and of no practical use. In a similar way, case stories about the cure of alcoholism and serious depressions are merely propaganda. Any well-trained professional knows better. Further protests by your rival about detailed case interviews should be blotted out as grotesques.

Bye the bye, if he starts exclaiming about the high pressure, hypnoticlike power that Andi teaches, insist he keep that secret. It is Machiavellian.

Be assured that Andi's book can only spoil your rival's well-established understanding. Reading it should be forbidden to all but the most naive.

Last and at least, do not read it yourself. It will wake you right up, and then your family will complain.

CARL A. WHITAKER, M.D.

Department of Psychiatry
University of Wisconsin–Madison

Preface

This book is the fruit of eight years of work with families with so-called psychiatric problems. Getting to know families in different countries, with different social and cultural backgrounds, and belonging to different ethnic and religious groups, has greatly broadened my professional experience and deepened my understanding of human and sociopolitical aspects of the family. In observing the dynamics of such diverse family groups, I have learned that although the circumstances that create distress in families can vary considerably, the problems, conflicts, and contradictions that arise are universal. In differing forms, we can all find them in our own families.

I have almost invariably found that the *disturbance* manifested in a person or a group is not the real problem at all. The apparent disturbance, in fact, usually reflects an underlying need for autonomy, a request for attention, a desire to rebel, a state of depression, etc. But the distress experienced by the person or group actually derives from the *significance* attributed to the disturbance. For example, anorexia, delirium, depression, and encopresis take on different meanings according to how one looks at them. If they are seen as signs of *mental disturbances* in individuals, then one will study the patient and look for the causes of the disturbance within him. His disturbance will be classified, which stabilizes it so that it eventually becomes irreversible, while its interactional significance and the influence of the social context in which it has arisen is ignored. In this way, society and the family isolate, stigmatize, and confound the individual by failing to consider all of the elements that contribute to the creation and maintenance of a given behavior.

In this book I have tried to give a simple, comprehensible description of systems theory and its applications in interactional therapy. My

experience in treating families and my teaching activities* have persuaded me to write a book about family therapy in the hope of stimulating reflection and criticism among others who work in the mental health
professions. In order to present the material as clearly as possible, I have
limited my field of study to one system—the family—although in reality
we cannot analyze one system without examining its relations to the
other systems that interact with it.

This is a technical book in the sense that it deals with the specifics of
therapy. It represents an attempt to "translate" and apply to the Italian
context theories and clinical experiences that have been developed in the
United States during the last two decades. In particular, this book proposes the systems model as an alternative approach with which Italian
mental health workers can confront their own approach to intervention.

I think that the family system represents the basic field for the development of an interactional approach. Once this approach has been
assimilated, we can go beyond the confines of the family group to
explore the dialectic, circular relationships between the family and other
more complex social systems.

Doing therapy *with* the family forces us to recognize the contradictions, roles, and social stereotypes that influence both the family group
and the therapeutic team. This recognition leads us to examine
modalities of communication that are often based on stereotyped patterns and rigid sexual and familial roles that impede the process of
change that is already taking place on other levels in our society.

Family therapy gives back to the identified patient his capacity for
self-determination within a changed family context. When a family's latent capacities for self-healing are rediscovered and activated, disturbed
behavior is seen no longer as a stigma but as a *signal* and an opportunity
for growth in a group with a history. In this modified context, all family
members are freer to participate more fully in the life of the community.

MAURIZIO ANDOLFI
Rome, Italy

---

*Both family treatment and my teaching activities are carried out at the Family Therapy Institute
(Rome, Via Reno 30) and, to a lesser extent, at the Institute of Child Psychiatry at the University
of Rome.

Acknowledgments

I want first of all to thank all those who have taken part in our family therapy training program for having encouraged me with their enthusiasm and constructive criticisms. I am particularly indebted to my personal collaborators, Paolo Menghi, Anna Nicolò, and Carmine Saccu, with whom I founded the Italian Society for Family Therapy in 1974. Their collaboration over the past years has helped me deepen and extend my knowledge of the family and of interactional therapy, and their contribution to the elaboration of this book has been invaluable.

I also wish to acknowledge my gratitude to those people who have most deeply influenced my work: Salvador Minuchin and Jay Haley, who profoundly impressed me with their wealth of ideas, clinical experience, and teaching ability during the period in which I worked at the Philadelphia Child Guidance Clinic; Kitty Laperriere of the Nathan Ackerman Family Institute, New York, and Andy Ferber of the Albert Einstein College in New York, for their attention to the process of personal and group growth of family therapists; Israel Zwerling, who taught me to reconsider the family in the context of the community; Helen De Rosis of the Karen Horney Clinic, New York, for my personal analysis; and Luigi Cancrini, with whom I initiated my work in family therapy in 1969 and who encouraged me to study the methodology of interactional therapy.

Most of all I am grateful to my brother Silvano and to my family of origin It was within my own family, with its long and painful experience of "mental illness," that I learned to understand and respect qualities such as courage, dedication, sacrifice, and the will to change, and to appreciate how difficult it is to protect these qualities from irrational fears, anguish, weakness, and stereotypes.

I wish to express my appreciation to my wife, Marcella, who has always supported me and enriched me with her extraordinary sensitivity and courage.

Finally, my thanks are due to Katia Giacometti, one of my most brilliant students, for her help in revising this book for the American edition, and to Bobbie Cassin, for undertaking the arduous task of translating it.

Contents

Introduction

The Family as an Interactional System

Premises

In a systemic approach, human beings and events are studied in terms of their interactions rather than their intrinsic characteristics. The theoretical bases for studying phenomena in this way are in sharp contrast with the mechanistic causal view that has dominated our culture and influenced our mode of thought for centuries.

To affirm that the behavior of one individual is the cause of another's behavior is to apply an over-simplified conceptual model that artificially reduces the complexities of reality to linear relations of cause and effect. For example, to say that a child behaves "badly" at school because his family has not brought him up properly is a statement based on a linear interpretation of reality (inadequate training at home→bad behavior at school). The formulation of problems in terms of cause and effect is the result of an arbitrary punctuation of a circular situation, which isolates an event from the sequence of events that precede and follow it.

From a systemic point of view, pharmacological or psychotherapeutic interventions that postulate a "sick" individual as the object of therapy are arbitrarily circumscribed. This is true of many approaches that have been developed in working with children and adolescents, where the individual is observed in isolation from his interactional context.

In fact, family therapy has been viewed with considerable skepti-

1

cism in the field of child psychiatry[1] both in America, where it originated, and in Europe. In Italy in particular, child psychiatry has traditionally emphasized analysis of the intrapsychic conflicts and personality problems of the child, usually excluding observation of the child's
familial and social relations as irrelevant or of only theoretical interest.

Nor have the Italian child guidance clinics attained markedly different results. Although in some cases these clinics do undertake an
analysis of the child's context, their work is handicapped by the frag-
mentary nature of their interventions and the rigid hierarchical structure
of their staffs. Theoretical and arbitrary compilations of data often substitute for real comprehension of the needs of the child and his family.

In general in the Italian public health services, very little is done in
the way of gathering information or directly observing the context[2] in
which particular behavior has originated; nor is an effort made to redefine the problems presented by their clients. Since the majority of mental health professionals are convinced that "disturbed" behavior can be
explained by considering the child or adult who manifests it as "sick,"
interpersonal aspects of the problem are usually ignored.

Consequently, the individual in difficulty becomes the *object* of observation. His "sick" or "deviant" behavior is scrutinized minutely, and
a diagnosis is made. A therapy is then chosen according to the requirements of the situation. It may consist of drugs, counseling, or intensive
individual psychotherapy. But whatever choice is made will be influenced by the original diagnostic approach that isolates the "sick" organism from its context of significant relations.

Crisis interventions are usually limited to hospitalization or pharmacological containment. In fact, these appear to be the *only* responses

---

[1]Particular attention will be given throughout this book to work done with children and
adolescents. In my opinion, success in family therapy depends on intervening early
enough in the development of "pathological" behavior, while the system is still capable of
transformation.

[2]Recent sociopsychological research has brought us to recognize the fundamental importance of the context in which communication occurs. Speech, relationships, attitudes, and
moods have significance with respect to a specific situation. By *situation* we mean the
particular circumstances that surround one or more persons at a given moment and influence their behavior. If these circumstances are ignored, we risk attributing a completely
different significance to a behavior, or we may consider it abnormal, crazy, bad, absurd,
delinquent, etc. The more rigid and conventional the observer's outlook, the more incomprehensible the behavior will seem. "Anyone who brushed his teeth in a busy street
rather than in his bathroom might be quickly carted off to a police station or to a lunatic
asylum" (Watzlawick, Beavin, & Jackson, 1967).

possible once it is taken for granted that the problem exists *in* an individual rather than *between* individuals. Attention is focused exclusively on the superficial aspect of the situation (the disturbed or disturbing behavior), without reference to the function of this behavior in the interactional system in which it occurs. Moreover, the psychiatrist's intervention tends to sanction the stigmatization of the individual in distress, to make the symptom chronic, and to crystallize the system of family relations around it.

In an alternative approach, the individual is observed in an interactional context (family, school, neighborhood, clan, etc.) in which his "different" behavior has a specific meaning. Investigation begins by analyzing the relationships existing *here* and *now* between the individual and his interactional system.

This kind of analysis has often been criticized for failing to take into consideration the individual's past history. Such criticism is superficial, however. An analysis of the significant relations existing among the component parts of a system at a given moment inevitably leads the investigator to correlate the observed data with the system's historical evolution. Moreover, the resulting reconstruction of the system's development will provide far more information than would an etiological study.

When we consider the family as an interactional system, we see it as something greater than the sum of individual behaviors. The family system includes these behaviors, and it articulates them in a functional whole.

In shifting from an individual to a systemic orientation, however, interventions are not always consistent with their theoretical premises. For example, in family therapy, the other systems that interact with the family, such as school, work, neighborhood, and friends, are sometimes ignored. The prospects opened up by a systemic interpretation of behavior are certainly encouraging, but in our enthusiasm for this undeniably effective approach, certain dangers still exist. For instance, the persistence of a linear logic can lead us to blame the family for causing the difficulties of one of its members. The family will then be considered "sick," rather than the individual patient. These pitfalls exist despite the fact that this approach and the theory behind it are based on the concept of circular causality.

These dangers have been pointed out by Salvador Minuchin (1970), who observed that "family therapy's focus is necessarily wider than that of child psychiatry, but even family therapy has tended to limit its interventions to the family, without extending its field of intervention to the school, the neighborhood, or in some cases, even the extended family."

With reference to this same problem, Auerswald (1972) divides family therapists into three categories:

1. Those who use a traditional linear causal model
2. Those who use an ecological model
3. Those who are in a transitional phase from the first to the second

He then considers an ecological view in connection with training programs for family therapists:

> The best way I know to expose interested people to situations in which they will begin to think as ecologists, is to throw them into an urban ghetto with the task of figuring out what to do for families in distress, while simultaneously creating an information environment for them which contains what we know about individuals and about families and other social systems, and including a view of general systems theory, cybernetics, information theory, cultural anthropology, kinesics, general and social ecology, human territoriality.

Here Auerswald emphasizes that in order to learn a systemic approach, the therapist in training must work in direct contact with the community. Theoretical knowledge of transactional processes has to be implemented by experience in the field. The breakdown of the traditionally rigid division of professional roles that inevitably occurs in working in this highly complex context teaches the therapist to deal with new responsibilities and demands genuine competence and effectiveness.

If we want to promote new policies in our public mental health services, we must start by abandoning some of our ingrained ways of thinking. Real and consistent change in models of intervention can be attained only by making a clear and consistent choice between alternative conceptual models.

This problem has received a great deal of attention in Italian mental health services. The rise of an antipsychiatry movement in the 1960's marked the beginning of a profound crisis in which radically different views of mental illness and of the role of mental health professionals were proposed. The traditional concept of mental illness as an internal *attribute* of the individual, independent of his significant relations with others, was finally rejected. The image of the mental health professional as a technician and agent of social control was challenged, as were traditional methods of treatment leading to the stigmatization and isolation of the disturbed individual (Basaglia, 1968).

The many constructive proposals that emerged during this period of intense debate eventually led to the acceptance of a new conception of mental disturbance and to the creation of alternative services, such as mental health centers.

The results of these innovations, however, have been disappointing. Generally speaking, there have been changes in form, not substance, because the concept of mental disturbance has been redefined within the framework of the traditional causal view of reality. The "cause" of mental illness is now sought elsewhere, but the underlying premises remain unaltered. Unfortunately, the persistence of the traditional conceptual framework often makes it difficult to recognize those innovations that do exist in the type of intervention and in the "alternative" way of working in these services.

The work done by nontraditional mental health professionals is frequently undermined by this lack of coherence and by a tendency toward oversimplification. For example, in redefining the patient-therapist relationship, the practice of delegating all responsibility to "the expert" is abandoned. But it is not enough to reject the patient's request that his problems be solved for him. The therapist must also know how to restore to the disturbed individual or system the capacity to deal adequately with his or its own problems.

The major problem now facing the nontraditional mental health professionals is to attain consistency in their interventions. This book emphasizes the need for a fundamental change in premises and proposes a systemic model as an alternative theoretical framework and as a stimulus to reflection on and criticism of our present way of working.

Interactional family therapy, when it is correctly conducted in a community context, is a form of social psychiatry.[3] In intervening in a single family, the therapist uncovers the major conflicts among its members, thereby eliminating the need for a scapegoat. In intervening simultaneously in the community, he exposes the conflictual aspects of the family's interactions with other significant social groups. This twofold intervention prevents the family and other social groups from refusing

---

[3]Community psychiatry is not an end in itself. It is only an instrument in the struggle to eliminate the labeling, alienation, and oppression of people suffering from psychiatric disturbances.

responsibility by arbitrarily scapegoating one component of a complex interactional network.

To some extent, the particular attention given to the family in preference to other systems reflects an arbitrary and subjective choice. But this choice is based on the recognition that "the family as a socializing unit is antecedent to schools, youth movements, adolescent gangs or peer groups as a mediator between what is individual, innate and private and that which is social, cultural and public" (Hochmann, 1971). In reality, the family represents only one point of entrance to an ecosystem. The family is chosen as the field of intervention only after carefully assessing the complex network of interactions present in and among the various systems of which the individual is a part.

In family therapy, relationships between individual behavior and the family group are analyzed within a broader conceptual framework derived from systems theory and communication theory. Reality is seen as a totality of interacting systems. In observing human interaction, we apply the same principles and deductions as are valid for the study of systems in general.[4]

The scope of a systemic investigation differs from that of a traditional psychological study. In a systemic investigation, the internal structure of the single, isolated unit becomes irrelevant. What matters is what happens between the units that compose the system, that is, how changes in one unit are preceded or followed by changes in the other units.

According to Bertalanffy (1969), *every organism is a system, a dynamic ordering of parts and processes that interact reciprocally*. Adopting this perspective, we consider the family an open system composed of units that are held together by rules of behavior and by dynamic functions, and that interact with each other and with an external context. In fact, we consider every social group a system composed of multiple microsystems in reciprocal, dynamic interaction.

Our basic premise, therefore, is that the family is a system among systems and that the exploration of the interpersonal relations and norms that regulate the life of the significant groups to which the individual belongs is essential to an understanding of the behavior of the members and to the formulation of effective interventions.

---

[4]For a detailed exposition of systems theory, see Bertalanffy, *General System Theory* (1969), and Watzlawick *et al.*, *Pragmatics of Human Communication* (1967).

TOWARD A REDEFINITION OF DIAGNOSIS AND INTERVENTION

To see how this new method of interpretation and analysis can contribute to a revision of premises and practices, we should examine three postulates of systems theory as applied to the family.

The Family as a System in Continual Transformation

The family is a system that adapts to the changing demands of the different phases of its developmental cycle as well as to changes in the demands of society. It must adapt in order to provide its members with both continuity and opportunity for psychosocial growth (Minuchin, 1974).

The family achieves this twofold scope by attaining a dynamic equilibrium between two seemingly contradictory functions: a *tendency toward homeostasis* and a *capacity for transformation*. Feedback loops operate by means of complex mechanisms to maintain the system's homeostasis (negative feedback) or else to produce change (positive feedback).

It has been found that negative feedback mechanisms are particularly important in families with psychiatric problems. In fact, this discovery marked a turning point in the development of family therapy. In family systems where pathological behavior has become consolidated in one of the members, there is a tendency to repeat certain transactions in an almost automatic way. These transactions conform to rigid rules that serve to maintain the system's homeostasis:

> Such a model for family interaction was proposed by Jackson when he introduced the concept of *family homeostasis*. Observing that the families of psychiatric patients often demonstrated drastic repercussions (depression, psychosomatic disorders and the like) when the patient improved, he postulated that these behaviors and perhaps therefore the patient's illness as well were homeostatic mechanisms operating to bring the disturbed system back into its delicate balance. (Watzlawick *et al.*, 1967)

Unfortunately, the concept of homeostasis has at times been inflated and utilized inappropriately. Misunderstanding of this concept has led to reduced expectations concerning the capacity of "disturbed families" to change. As a result, therapy has often led to a strengthening of the *status quo* rather than to the activation of the family's creative potentials.[5]

---

[5]"There is also a learning and growth in the family, and it is exactly here that a pure homeostasis model errs most, for these effects are closer to *positive* feed-back. The differ-

This tendency to overemphasize the importance of homeostatic processes has been completely reversed by Buckley. In Buckley's view, positive feedback mechanisms are responsible for all growth, innovation, and creativity in social systems (in Speer, 1970).

Actually, neither homeostatic tendencies nor tendencies toward change are intrinsically good or bad. Moralistic judgements are inappropriate as well as arbitrary and indicate failure to really understand what is meant by the definition of the family as a system in continual transformation. The concept of a family life cycle implies that the relationship between continuity and change has to be assessed in relation to the successive phases of a total developmental cycle.

It also means that rigidity and flexibility (the capacity to adjust to internal or external requirements) are not intrinsic characteristics of a system. With respect to an entire family life cycle, moreover, positive and negative feedback are really aspects of a single process.

The Family as an Active Self-Regulating System

The family structures its interactions according to rules that it has developed and modified through trial and error over a period of time. By means of these rules, the family members learn what is permitted and what is forbidden in a relationship until a stable definition of the relationship evolves. This process leads to the creation of a systemic whole that is maintained by specific transactional patterns[6] potentially capable of being modified.

Families, like other human organisms, are not passive recipients but

---

entiation of behavior, reinforcement and learning (of both adaptive and symptomatic behavior), and the ultimate growth and departure of children all indicate that while from one view the family is balanced by homeostasis, on the other hand, there are important simultaneous factors of change in the operation, and a model of family interaction must incorporate these and other principles into a more complex configuration" (Watzlawick *et al.*, 1967).

[6]"Transactional patterns regulate family members' behavior. They are maintained by two systems of constraint. The first is generic, involving the universal rules governing family organization. For instance, there must be a power hierarchy, in which parents and children have different levels of authority. There must also be a complementarity of functions, with the husband and wife accepting interdependency and operating as a team. The second system of constraint is idiosyncratic, involving the mutual expectations of particular family members. The origin of these expectations is buried in years of explicit and implicit negotiations among family members, often around small daily events" (Minuchin, 1974).

intrinsically active systems. What Bertalanffy (1969) says about active organisms in general is also true of families: "A stimulus (for example, a change in external conditions) does not *cause* a process to occur in an otherwise inert system; it merely modifies processes already existing in an autonomously active system."

In the same way, any form of stress, originating in changes either within the family (births, departures, divorces, deaths) or outside of the family (changes in residence or job, changes in values) influence family functioning and require a process of adaptation. In other words, both intrasystemic and extrasystemic changes require a continual transformation of transactional patterns if the family is to maintain continuity and still allow its members to grow. It is during periods of inter- or intrasystemic change or stress that the majority of so-called psychiatric problems arise.

It is important to keep in mind the profound transformations that have taken place in our social system in less than a decade. Particularly striking are the increased importance of the group with respect to the individual; the radical change in marital roles and functions; the progressive disintegration of the extended patriarchal family and the greater autonomy and differentiation experienced in the nuclear family; the new attitudes toward having children, etc. These vast transformations make it necessary to search for new equilibriums between homeostatic tendencies and desire for change.

When a family group is already in a precarious situation, this search for a new equilibrium can lead to decompensation or to greater rigidity, thereby creating stress in an individual, in the couple, or most often, among the children.

With these factors in mind, the mental health professional's first objective is to assess correctly the incidence of "disturbing" factors capable of provoking decompensation in family functioning. It is clear that psychiatric diagnoses or therapies that implicitly label the individual in distress (while ignoring the social context and the internal and external sources of stress) merely contribute to the problem. Moreover interventions of this kind can be particularly harmful because they are presented as solutions to the problem.[7]

---

[7]"Under certain circumstances problems will arise purely as the result of wrong attempts at changing an existing difficulty. . . . Or, more absurdly still, even a nonexistent difficulty" (Watzlawick, Weakland, & Fisch, 1974).

The Family as an Open System in Interaction with Other Systems

The family system interacts with a variety of other social systems such as schools, factories, neighborhoods, and peer groups. Extrafamilial relationships, therefore, have to be observed within the context of the family's whole network of social relationships. These extrafamilial relationships influence and are in turn influenced by the norms and values of society.

Lévi-Strauss has described the relations between a social group and the families that compose it in terms of a dynamic equilibrium. He has pointed out that these relationships are not static, like the relationship between a wall and the bricks of which it is made. Instead, it is "a dynamic process involving tension and contrast. It is extremely difficult to locate a center of equilibrium, because its exact location is subject to infinite variations which depend on time and on society."

In examining the family in terms of its extrafamilial relations, we are once again reminded of the danger of oversimplifying reality. Our field of investigation should not be limited to the individual in the context of his family system but should include the complex network of relationships that surround the family microsystem.

If we consider all of these premises, it becomes clear why shifting from an individual to a family approach means more than just substituting one field of study and intervention with another. It means adopting an entirely different conceptual model, which leads us to "see" an entirely different world. The inner world of intrapsychic processes is replaced by a world of interactive behaviors, observed in their spatial and temporal context.

The attitude of the researcher or therapist working in this framework changes. He does not attempt to *explain* an individual, whom he sees in isolation, by making inferences about him. He becomes a participant in an active process, and he is no longer primarily concerned with interpreting phenomena. Many concepts—such as behavior, personality, and character, as well as traditional therapeutic premises concerning diagnosis, change, intervention, etc.—are redefined from a systemic point of view.

For example, personality or behavior (including pathological behavior) is no longer thought of as an attribute of the individual. These are terms that describe characteristics that *come into being* through repeated interactional experiences. The behavior of an individual is a signal of the relationship existing in a particular phase of the family life cycle, between his needs for autonomy and differentiation and the rigidity or elasticity of the rules in his family system.

Disturbed behavior is a signal that needs for autonomy and differentiation have been sacrificed to maintain dysfunctional familial relations. A family system becomes dysfunctional when it does not have the capacity or the means for assimilating change or, in other words, when the rigidity of its rules prevents it from adjusting to its own life cycle and to that of the individual.

To stabilize a dysfunctional system, a great deal of energy must be invested in maintaining the rigid rules and stereotyped roles that limit family transactions to repetitive patterns. Dysfunction and rigidity therefore become synonymous. Yet, rigidity and flexibility are not qualities that are intrinsic in a system. These, too, are descriptive terms used by an observer to indicate the degree of difficulty that a family encounters in a particular phase of its cycle of development, when it is faced with the problem of finding a new dynamic equilibrium between its unifying function and its members' needs for growth and differentiation— that is, between continuity and change.

Symptomatic behavior is a signal of the rigid structuring of family relationships. It protects an equilibrium that has been constructed around a conflictual situation (which thereby becomes functional). This apparent equilibrium, maintained by monopolizing the energies present in the system, prevents all of the members (not only the identified patient) from gradually working out ways of reconciling personal needs with interactive requirements. Consequently, each member feels endangered by the emergence of new situations or needs related to his individual development or to that of the system.

Once disturbed behavior is redefined in this way, traditional diagnostic categories no longer serve any purpose. Instead of classifying an individual's behavior, we try to decipher the meaning of this behavior in terms of the context in which it occurs. Diagnosis, therefore, becomes the assessment of the function of a symptom within a family system. To evaluate a symptom in these terms, the therapist focuses on the relationship that exists between the self and its individual functioning and the self and the family's functioning.

We have not yet described the position of the therapist in the diagnostic process. In practice, in order to assess the state of a system, we have to take into consideration the relationship between the self and the function of the therapist, and the self and the function of each family member. In other words, evaluation must include an analysis of the *therapeutic system*. In an interactional approach, it is impossible to assess a family system independently from the family-therapist relationship.

Furthermore, since assessment concerns the degree of rigidity or flexibility of the system (and therefore its capacity to change), diagnosis and intervention can be distinguished only on a theoretical level. In fact, the best way of discovering to what extent a family is open to change is to see how the family reacts to the therapist's interventions. In this kind of situation, the therapist is neither a neutral observer nor the activator of an otherwise inert system.

The position of the therapist becomes clearer if we consider the problem of change. Change is seen in terms of the liberation and re-channeling of the energies existing in a system so that they can be utilized for self-therapeutic purposes; that is, so that they can be directed toward the *active* exploration of new personal and interactive areas. This view of change implies another complete break with the traditional premises of therapy. It requires the creation of a context that facilitates confrontation among the members of a family and encourages them to interact in ways that differ from their usual patterns.

In the traditional view of intervention, derived from a medical model, change depends on the skill of the therapist or on the miraculous effects of scientific knowledge. In a systemic view, the therapist's intervention is based on a systemic analysis of the family's problems and on the activation of the family's self-therapeutic potentials. The family takes charge of its own interactional problems as these are gradually brought to light, so that the family itself becomes the protagonist of the therapeutic process.

To achieve this goal, the therapist must bring to therapy not only his full store of technical experience but his own personality, imagination, sense of humor, and ability to share others' emotions as well. And he has to give up his role as a healer.[8]

Therapist and family are two active systems. Their encounter creates a third system, called the *therapeutic system*. The therapist is an active participant in this system and abandons the position of an outside expert. Each member of the system participates equally in working out

---

[8]"When the therapist allows himself to become a healer or repairman, the family goes into dysfunction to wait for the therapist to accomplish his work" (Bowen, 1966).

rules that enable both family and therapist to explore new transactional patterns.

The role of the therapist is therefore completely redefined: his objective is to unbalance the equilibrium of the system and of each of its members in order to activate the system's inherent capacity to evolve new forms of encounter and participation.

The ultimate goal of therapy is the attainment of a new equilibrium between self and function on an individual and on a systemic level. This goal is reached through a process of exploration in which the family plays the leading part. Therapy creates a context that enables the members of the system to experience new ways of interacting through the mediation of the therapist, who acts initially as a *consultant* on the family problems and later as a *supervisor* of the family's efforts.

In this way the therapist can utilize his skills to restore competence to the family system, so that the family can become the protagonist in its own process of growth.

1

Formation of the Therapeutic System

THE THERAPEUTIC TEAM

The Setting

I think it is important to describe the physical characteristics of the setting and some of the basic procedures we use in working with families[1] before analyzing the process of therapy itself.

The therapeutic setting consists in a rather large therapy room with few but essential furnishings: chairs arranged in a circle, a blackboard, a small bookcase, and a large box of toys that is always available when we have families with children. There is a one-way mirror and sound equipment that enable supervisor and observers[2] to see and hear what is going on from the next room.

We also have a television camera with which we can film sessions. The film can then be viewed and analyzed by the therapeutic team or by the family itself on closed-circuit television. Audio visual equipment is also extremely useful for training purposes. It enables the trainee to observe the patterning of family interaction, the congruence of verbal and analogic messages, the use of space and its pragmatic significance, etc.—with an immediacy and sense of the here-and-now of a situation

---

[1] I am referring to work with families carried out in Rome at the Center for Research on Communication in Systems and, to a lesser extent, at the Institute of Child Psychiatry of the University of Rome.

[2] We also conduct training programs in family therapy, The observers are usually students who are learning how to observe in systemic terms.

that could not be conveyed in any other way. It teaches the future therapist to "see" in systemic terms, and it demonstrates objectively just how difficult the art of therapy really is.

We often find it very useful to play back[3] the material filmed during the earlier sessions. We watch the film with the family and then discuss it together.

We used this technique with the Tozzi family, who came to therapy because of their daughter's mutism. No progress was being made despite the mother's continual efforts to induce the daughter to speak. Every time the girl was about to take some initiative or was simply about to open her mouth, her mother jumped in and substituted for her. The girl then hesitated more, and the mother reacted by encouraging her more actively. The vicious circle went on endlessly. If the husband criticized the mother in any way, the situation became even more rigid.

When a sequence like this is seen on the television screen, the mother has an opportunity to see for herself that her encouragement is actually inhibiting her daughter rather than helping her. Once she has realized this fact, she may be able to visualize a different solution and therefore seek new ways of interacting.

Playing back filmed material also helps transform the "family system" into a "therapeutic system" by engaging family and therapist in a common task.

We inform the family about our equipment and procedures during the first session. Usually, the family has no difficulty in accepting them, despite their intrusive character. We find that within a very short time, the family tends to forget that it is being heard, observed, and perhaps even filmed.[4] During the course of therapy the family eventually comes to regard the presence of supervisor and the observers as a sign of the therapeutic team's commitment to help in finding a solution to their problem.

Children are often curious about the mirror and want to know what can be seen from behind it. We accompany them into the observation room and let them talk to the supervisor and other members of the team.

---

[3]Playing back registered material during therapy provides feedback to the family system, so that the system can correct or modify its behaviors and visualize alternative solutions (Alger, 1973).

[4]We ask each family's written authorization to film the sessions. In turn, we guarantee that the films will be shown only for professional purposes, and we describe how we use this material in furthering therapeutic progress.

Sometimes some members of the family are asked to observe from behind the mirror while the rest of the family is engaged in some activity.[5] At other times, the supervisor may decide to intervene directly. He joins the therapist in the therapy room and temporarily works together with him on some specific objective.

In other words, the one-way mirror acts as a permeable diaphragm between the family-therapist system, which is directly involved in action in the therapy room, and the supervisor-observer system. The latter, less emotionally involved, analyzes the sequences of communication that occur between family and therapist and can more easily comprehend the ongoing action in its totality. It is amazing to what extent the mirror creates *distance* from the emotional climate prevailing in the therapy room. It is this *distance* that enables an observer to identify redundant communication[6] and nonverbal messages, as well as possible errors on the part of the therapist.

Selvini, Boscolo, Cecchin, and Prata (1978) feel that the presence of the supervisor is essential to the success of therapy with families characterized by schizophrenic transactions. Selvini observed that these families easily manage to entangle the therapist in their pathological rules of behavior. It seems to me, however, that this danger is always present—with any kind of family. I am convinced that the therapist-supervisor combination is preferable in all brief, strategic therapies.

The Therapist-Supervisor Relationship

The success of brief, strategic therapies relies in large part on the therapist-supervisor relationship. The quality of the relationship formed in the sessions between the therapist and the family reflects the relationship between the therapist and his supervisor. Whether the supervisor has more experience than the therapist (as, for example, in a training situation) or whether there is no substantial difference in this respect,

---

[5] I will discuss this aspect of therapy again in later chapters in connection with strategies involving the division of the family into subsystems.

[6] Repetitive sequences of communication are called *pragmatic redundancies*. For example, if B invariably follows A, then B is redundant. The fact that A invariably accepts that B follows A is also redundant. This kind of sequence indicates the presence of a specific rule of behavior: "An extreme circumscription of possible behaviors along any particular dimension into one redundant configuration is observed, which prompted Jackson further to characterize families as rule-governed systems" (Watzlawick, Beavin, & Jackson, 1967).

mutual respect and adaptability must exist. Therapist and supervisor have equally important roles in therapy, but their separate responsibilities must be clearly defined.

Their functions are complementary, like those of a coach and a player during a football game. The coach observes the overall trend of the game and watches the player's moves in relation to those of the other players. He can offer the player suggestions that can be particularly helpful if made at the right moment. In the same way, the supervisor's field of observation includes both therapist and family, so that he is in a good position to offer advice on how to create and maintain a cooperative atmosphere. He suggests moves to the therapist in accordance with the overall plan of the therapy. It is the therapist's job to put the suggestions into effect, while keeping in mind the moves of the family members and the actual situation existing at a particular moment. Although the therapist follows the supervisor's instructions, he maintains his freedom of intervention. In fact, a valid therapeutic relationship depends on the therapist's free use of his own personality and his individual sensitivity.

If the therapist-supervisor pair is to function well, both partners have to be prepared to resolve the problems that inevitably arise whenever two people work together. We reserve considerable time for discussing an ongoing therapy both before and after each session. The whole team may join in discussing strategies, formulating prescriptions, exchanging personal reactions, assessing the effectiveness of the supervisor's instructions, observing the families' counterreactions, etc.

During the actual sessions, therapist and supervisor can communicate with each other directly by interphone. Or, whenever the therapist feels it is necessary, he leaves the therapy room to exchange information and assess the situation together with the supervisor. Leaving the room also permits the therapist to free himself momentarily from his emotional involvement in the session.[7]

The chief difference between direct and indirect supervision is that in the former, the supervisor actually sees what is happening in the therapy room; consequently, his suggestions are more effective because they can be acted on immediately. This also makes it possible to correct

---

[7]"The most basic assumption of all is that any family can absorb and orient the therapist and direct him away from his functions as a change agent; that any therapist can be caught behaving with the family in ways that will reinforce the very patterns that brought them to therapy" (Montalvo, 1973).

therapeutic mistakes that might otherwise increase the family's distress.

A therapist-supervisor combination also differs from a co-therapy arrangement where two therapists work together in the therapy room. In working with a therapist-supervisor model, we find that it can be useful in some cases to use a member of the family as a *temporary co-therapist*. We may use one of the parents, the identified patient, an adolescent, or even a grandparent. This kind of *ad hoc* co-therapy can be extremely effective. Sometimes it is more advantageous to have a co-therapist inside the family system than outside of it. Finding a co-therapist among the family members represents a decided step forward in therapy and indicates that the therapist has been fully accepted into the system.

THE FIRST SESSION

The importance of the first session cannot be overstated. The therapist's first encounter with the family system is paradigmatic for an understanding of an interactional approach. The primary objective is to create the conditions that enable therapist and family to formulate a correct therapeutic contract. Therefore, the therapist's initial concern is to create a favorable atmosphere for gathering information.

In planning therapy, the therapist needs an accurate *map* of the family's interactional structure. He pieces together a map by eliciting information and identifying the family's interpersonal boundaries, functional and dysfunctional areas, etc.

The map that the therapist constructs is really a chart that describes a particular phase in the family's development. According to Minuchin (1974), a map is merely a scheme of the family's organization:

> It does not represent the richness of family transactions any more than a map represents the richness of a territory. It is static, whereas the family is constantly in motion. But the family map is a powerful simplification device, which allows the therapist to organize the diverse material that he is getting. The map allows him to formulate hypotheses about areas within the family that function well and about other areas that may be dysfunctional.

The therapist's decision about with whom to intervene and what strategy to adopt will depend on which systems and subsystems he thinks are involved in maintaining the presenting problem. He must carefully evaluate which elements will be of most use in working out a solution.

The therapist needs to learn how the system is structured and how it functions *here* and *now* in the encounter between family and therapist. In an interactional therapy, intervention does not depend directly on diagnosis. Since the therapist takes an active part in constructing the family map, he includes himself in it. Therefore, what emerges is really a *map of the therapeutic system*. In other words, in evaluating the family, its transactions are not assessed in a void but in relation to the therapeutic team. The more the therapist is able to observe and to let himself be observed, the easier it will be to formulate a therapeutic contract based on a clear definition of the relationship between the family and the therapeutic team.

The therapist has to keep in mind that the therapeutic context places limitations on the behavior of all the persons involved and that his own behavior can reinforce dysfunctional relations. The therapist-supervisor relationship provides a way of dealing with these difficulties. Whereas the therapist's job is to observe how the family responds to him, it is the job of the supervisor to observe how the therapist and the family respond to each other and to codify the information that emerges from their relationship.

What I want to stress is that in interactional therapy, diagnosis is a progressive matter and that in practice, diagnosis and intervention are part of a single process. On the one hand, a diagnosis emerges from the information that the family system provides with its responses to the therapist's actions. On the other hand, the therapist's interventions derive from hypotheses based on his initial observations of the family's interactional patterns and their degree of rigidity.

The therapist presents himself as a person "who wants to understand more." His observations are never definitive but must be constantly verified by actively exploring the system. This kind of exploration, which tests the family's willingness to try out new models of interaction, will indicate to the therapist how to amplify or modify the family map. These successive modifications guide him in formulating new interventions, which in turn allow him to gather further information.

A complete map of the family's relations is built up slowly and progressively. The more accurate the result, the more likely it is that the goals of therapy will be correctly defined when the therapeutic contract is formulated.

Initial Diagnostic Observations

The Preliminary Contact

In the majority of cases, some contact occurs before the first session. There may be a telephone call or a brief interview with one or more family members or perhaps with a social worker, a teacher, or some other person outside the family who has advised therapy. It rarely happens that the first contact occurs with the entire family group.

Whatever form the first contact takes, it provides the therapist with useful information that has to be analyzed in interactional forms. That is, whatever information is supplied by a family member or a social agency must be considered as one version of the problem—*not the problem*.

From the initial telephone call or the initial interview, the therapist gathers transactional as well as factual information about the family.

For example, the family member who telephones may be the one who is most highly motivated to undertake therapy, and he may be pulling other more reluctant members of the family along with him. Sometimes the person who calls tries to establish a coalition[8] with the therapist before even meeting him. This person will probably begin therapy feeling that he holds a special, privileged position and feeling entitled to act as the family's spokesman.

Or else the person tries to compete with the therapist. He may indicate, in various ways, that if the therapist wants to get to know the family, he will have to obey this person's rules. For example, he will want to decide which members of the family to bring to therapy, to fix the day and hour of the appointment, to tell the therapist what is really wrong with a child, etc.

Another person may want to communicate to the therapist that the situation is hopeless, that it is all the fault of a child or of the other spouse or of some past event and that he hopes that the therapist will officially confirm his opinions.

In other cases, the family member who telephones feels embarrassed about asking for therapy. He feels it is stigmatizing or that it represents a defeat for the family. Or else he expects miracles from the therapist and tries in this first contact to delegate all responsibility to the "expert," hoping to keep himself out of the situation.

[8]A coalition is "an agreement of alliance established for the mutual benefit of the allies vis-à-vis a third party" (Sluzki, 1975).

This kind of information allows the therapist to formulate hypotheses that he will try to verify when he meets the family. For instance, he will form some idea about the motivations behind the family's request for therapy and how these may influence the members' behavior at the first consultation. In particular, he will be able to make an initial assessment of the system's rigidity, on the basis of the family's efforts to manipulate the therapist before the first meeting.

As we can see, this preliminary phase can become a battle for control of the therapeutic relationship. If the therapist attempts to avoid this battle, he will risk creating a relationship of pseudomutuality with the family.

The Opening Phase of the First Session

In the opening phase, the therapist tries to make all of the family members feel comfortable and to make contact with each one. He invites them to sit down wherever they wish, and he informs them about the one-way mirror, the supervisor, and the observers and in general tries to make them familiar with the setting. He tries to create a confidential rather than a detached professional atmosphere. He then asks each person's name and presents a series of questions to stimulate everyone's participation.

Clearly, the form and timing of the therapist's efforts to make contact with the family and to gather information depend on the behavior of the family itself. In this phase, the family may recreate the same situation already proposed in the preliminary contact. For example, a family in crisis will probably want to talk about their problem immediately and ask the therapist to find a solution.

If the therapist hopes to create a viable therapeutic system, he has to redefine the problem in interactional terms as rapidly as possible, and he must restore the family to a responsible and active role in the therapeutic process.

The therapist uses different ways of contacting and gathering information from children than he uses with adults. His questions and his attitudes change, too, according to whether he is addressing a farmworker or a teacher, a rebellious adolescent or a frightened child, a proud mother or a frustrated housewife.

A family therapist has to learn to enter into the family's world, adapting his own language, personal style, and experiences to the particular people with whom he is dealing. He must also learn to respect the family's "rules" and to see the reality and needs of the family in its broader social framework.[9]

In this earliest phase, the therapist communicates to the family that each member is equally important and that he is interested in them as people and not only because they are experiencing difficulties. The discussion deals with neutral questions rather than with the problem that has brought the family to therapy. This is an effective way of creating a collaborative atmosphere and of presenting the first rule of therapy—that *each person is equally important and worthy of attention*.

In the interest of the family as a whole, it is the therapist's job to uphold this rule throughout therapy, by preventing or blocking any efforts to deviate from it.

While the therapist must enter into the family's world and adapt himself to it, the family must accept the rules of therapy. This concept of mutual accommodation is important, because it represents a concrete modality of encounter, and it makes everyone feel responsible for the success of a common task.

To summarize, in the opening phase of therapy, the therapist makes a series of observations on which he bases a preliminary diagnostic assessment of the system. This assessment guides his interventions so that a clear definition of the therapeutic relationship can be reached and so that the goals of the therapeutic contract can be correctly formulated.

How the Family Presents Itself

The family's attitude, where they sit, and the degree of congruence between their verbal and nonverbal communications are among the first things that the therapist notices. The therapist formulates his initial hypotheses about the type of system he is dealing with and about the relationship between personal and interactive space in the system.

One family may appear "frozen," with each member responding in

[9]A family therapist has to be familiar with the family's general socio-cultural background as well as the specific context in which its members live and work. In an interactional approach, the therapist begins by exploring the family's social context in order to identify those areas where intervention may be most opportune. This methodology can be particularly useful in community psychiatric services. This kind of work requires a knowledge of intersystemic relations as well as an adequate sociopolitical orientation if the therapist is to define a specific problem correctly and to plan an effective intervention.

monosyllables to the therapist's questions and long intervals of silence. Another family may seem friendly and pleased to find a confidential atmosphere: the children move around the room and start to play, feeling right at home. In still another family, one or both parents may feel that they have to talk immediately about the problem that is troubling them. In this case, the atmosphere soon becomes uncomfortable, and usually accusatory. In other cases, the therapist perceives that the identified patient has been brought to therapy with some strategem (this often happens to adolescents), and the parents have an air of complicity. There are also cases in which the therapist perceives that the family has not come spontaneously but has been sent by some outside authority (school, various institutions). These families are likely to be strongly defensive and suspicious.

These first observations allow the therapist to formulate hypotheses about the flexibility or rigidity of the system. The "frozen" family, in a hurry to describe the problem that they feel unable to solve, may lead the therapist to think that the system is very rigid. He will want to verify this in his future interventions, and he may eventually modify his initial hypothesis. For instance, he may discover that the family seems frozen because it has been referred to therapy by others; or that this is the way the family presents itself in any unfamiliar situation; or that the behavior of the family merely reflects the rigid attitude of the therapist, who is too static and fails to offer the family a different model of behavior.

Relations in and between Subsystems

The therapist follows up his first "superficial" observations with a more systematic exploration of the various subsystems. Further information confirms or modifies his initial impressions concerning the flexibility or rigidity of intrafamilial boundaries.

Relations between Parents and Children

Some parents are very strict with their children and worry about their manners (how they sit, the language they use, etc.). Others seem to ignore their children completely. At times, parents give the impression of being totally incompetent in coping with a child who behaves in a rebellious or bizarre way during the session. Many parents immediately comment on the differences between their "problem child" (whom they say is incompetent, insecure, and disappointing in his relationship to them) and another child who is "just the opposite" (competitive, self-confident, and a good son).[10]

The therapist notes how the children respond to their parents' requests and how the parents in turn initiate transactions with their children. The identified patient frequently asks his parents for confirmation (by a glance or a verbal suggestion, etc.) even when the therapist is merely asking him his name or inquiring about his classmates.

In children with bizarre behavior or very evident disturbances such as tics, stuttering, or stereotyped motor activity, these behaviors can become more pronounced and more frequent than usual during the sessions. Their frequency and intensity may vary greatly according to whether the parents are blaming the child or emphasizing some positive aspect of his personality.

If one of the children is disturbed, the parents often disagree on how to deal with the problem. Sometimes they disagree openly even in the first session; in other cases, the parents initially seem united and start to criticize each other only later on.

The parents may utilize one of the children, usually the identified patient, as a mediator in their relationship. That is, they communicate with each other by talking about their child. This enables each partner to criticize the other without endangering the marital relationship. For example, the father may be telling the therapist about his work, while mother and daughter wink and smile knowingly at each other, in complicity, as though to disqualify the father's claim to competence. Or else, while a wife is telling about herself, her husband gets "distracted" (he may start playing with their three-year-old child). What may seem to be completely casual behavior is repeated every time the therapist speaks to the wife. Noticing the behavior of this *triad*,[11] the therapist hypothesizes

[10]Vogel and Bell (1960) have written that the choice of a scapegoat is often based on the identification of a child with the parent he most resembles. Negative characteristics are perceived in the child even though the parent possesses these same qualities. Attention, however, is centered on the child, never on the parent. We frequently see a parent criticize a child for all of the characteristics that the parent rejects in the other spouse, to whom he cannot express his feelings directly.

[11]Jay Haley is the expert on human communications who has shed the most light on the significance of triads and on the profound change in perspective that occurs when we move from an analysis of the individual, to the dyad, and then to units of three or more people engaged in communicational sequences. The language we use to describe individuals or dyads is inadequate for the description of relations including three people. Dyadic relations, for example, can be described as symmetrical (when two people inter-

that the child is helping the mother and father by his "abnormal" behavior. For example, if the parents cannot be in a room together without fighting, then the child's fears serve to keep the parents separated and therefore have a protective function. By insisting that the problem is the child, the parents deflect their attention and the therapist's from their marital problems.

If a grandmother participates in the session, she may interfere in the parental relationship in questions concerning the children's education. Or else she may reinforce the father's position in the family with respect to the wife. Consequently, the wife will become distant and depressed, communicating that she feels left out of family affairs.

In reality, alliances and coalitions can be found in every family. The importance of observing and utilizing coalitionary processes in family therapy will become clearer in subsequent chapters.[12]

Relations between Siblings

It is also important to observe the interactions between children. Minuchin (1974) described the sibling subsystem as "the first social laboratory in which children can experiment with peer relationships. Within this context children support, isolate, scapegoat, and learn from each other."

Children's ability to play together, to share common interests, or to support each other vis-à-vis the adults indicates to what extent the "problem child" has been rigidly scapegoated. In general, the children's capacity for socializing among themselves is inversely proportional to the degree of tension present in the system. The therapist is particularly interested in observing the "distance" between the children and the rela-

---

act using the same type of behavior) or complementary (when the behavior of one completes the behavior of the other). But this terminology is inadequate to describe a unit made up of three people. To talk about a triad, we have to refer to coalitionary processes or of alliances between two persons directed against a third person. Once the interactional therapist has gone beyond an individual or dyadic analysis and is dealing with triads, he will automatically broaden his field of observation to include first the individual's familial context and then the larger unit consisting of the extended family and the larger social context.

[12]Concerning coalitions, Sluzki (1975) has written that "It is the *when* and the *how* of their formation that are critically significant; the structure, the sequential order, intensity, persistence, and style of coalitions observed during, or triggered by, a family interview provide key information in determining areas of family conflict, in discovering the family's homeostatic functions, and in orienting the treatment strategy."

tions between the parental and the sibling subsystems. This information enables him to make hypotheses about the extent of a child's intrusion into the parental territory and about his function as a deflector of parental confrontation.

Once the therapist is able to see the family as a system and has gathered information about the problem from both parents and children, he will have the basic elements he needs for judging, for example, whether the father will be capable of helping mother and child to separate from each other, or whether the other children can help in restoring the identified patient to the sibling subsystem.

Actually, exploring relations in and between subsystems serves two purposes. On the one hand, it is important in making diagnoses and predictions; on the other hand, it is a means of restructuring that in turn enables the therapist to obtain further information. Its importance in making diagnoses is easy to understand. In exploring the sibling system, for example, the therapist may find a parental child; or in examining the interactions within the parental subsystem, the therapist may identify a spouse conflict. It is also evident that restructuring interventions in separate subsystems help to clarify intrafamilial boundaries. For example, working with the sibling subsystem, the therapist can promote greater internal differentiation by distinguishing the adolescent children, with their need for autonomy, from the younger children, with their need for nurturing. We can see that this kind of exploration is also useful in prevention. In fact, by emphasizing the diverse needs of each child according to his age, the therapist can identify problems existing in each subgroup that might otherwise be concealed by the more "obvious" problems present in another subsystem.

The exploration of subsystems also underscores the need to define the limits of the problem that therapy will deal with. At the same time, by delimiting the problem, the therapist implicitly recognizes the relative "autonomy" of other particular needs evidenced in one or more subsystems. Therefore, a series of therapeutic contracts are formulated, each one focusing on a different problem. The successive solution of these problems constitutes the goal of the therapeutic process.

Relations between Family Members and the Therapist

The attitude of the children toward the therapist in this initial phase of therapy may reflect the way in which the parents have prepared them for the consultation. If a child is frightened by his first contact with the therapist, this fright may indicate that he feels he is being punished and may be abandoned. If the children are friendly and curious about the therapist and the setting, this attitude may indicate that the parents have presented the meeting as a pleasant event and that the parents are probably optimistic and will collaborate in therapy.

By observing the children, the therapist can also discover whether the family has been referred for consultation by some school authority (teacher, principal, psychologist). In these cases, the children, and the identified patient in particular, will probably react with nervousness and irritation from the very first moment.

I remember a case in which a 12-year-old boy turned the therapy room upside down while his parents completely ignored him. They seemed not to notice anything, indicating in this way their consent to the boy's destructive behavior.

Later in the session, when the therapist offered to help in establishing a more positive relationship between the school and the family (rejecting the school's labeling of Robert as a "character problem"), Robert finally stopped breaking toys, sat down between his parents, and joined the discussion. At the end of the discussion, the parents asked Robert to put the room back in order, thus demonstrating by a concrete gesture their willingness to cooperate in the plan agreed on in the session.

Even in this first contact, the therapist notices which family members implicitly or explicitly try to elicit his sympathy and interest. For instance, a mother may indicate that she wants to set up a special relationship with the therapist by showing him the results of the tests that a child has taken or by asking for an individual appointment or by answering for the children. The therapist has to be careful to avoid involvement in a coalition with her, thereby excluding the other family members.

Or again, the parents may look at their child with an expression of exasperation and then shift their gaze to the therapist as though asking him to agree with their views. They are inviting him to take sides with them "against" the child, and here, too, the therapist must avoid being drawn into a coalition, this time in a context of accusation.[13]

---

[13]With reference to the problem of the therapist's position vis-à-vis the coalitionary process, Sluzki (1975) wrote that "Regardless of his efforts, the therapist will simply not be able to avoid getting involved in negotiations about coalitions"; and that "the chief rule about coalitions is that the therapist is going to establish only shifting, instrumental coalitions without binding himself to stable, *aprioristic* ones or following the culturally estab-

Here again, in discussing the family-therapist relationship, the role of the supervisor is extremely important. His task is to make sure the therapist gathers the systemic information needed for formulating a correct therapeutic contract. In particular, the supervisor must be certain that the therapist obtains sufficient information concerning who was responsible for bringing the family to therapy and what the family's motivations are. This information will help the therapist avoid misinterpretations of the family's attitude toward therapy. Second, the supervisor must be sure that the therapist establishes direct contact with each family member. In particular, the therapist must avoid protecting the identified patient, thereby reinforcing his role as scapegoat. Third, the supervisor must note any emotional reactions the therapist may have toward some family member, so that he will not be led into a symmetrical relationship with one component of the system.

Exploring the Problem

How to Ask about the Problem

So far, in our description of a first session, we have taken for granted that the family in question leaves the therapist some possibility of making contact and exploring the problem area. This in itself represents an important element in evaluating the system's flexibility. In this situation, the therapist can examine the different versions of the problem proposed by the family members. He selects the definition that best permits him to verify his initial hypotheses and to obtain further information about the family's interactional patterns.

The therapist can begin by asking, "What is your problem?" Formulated in this way, the question seems directed to the entire family, and it defines a situation in which people are expected to talk about the problem that motivated the visit. Using an open-ended question, the therapist is probably interested in seeing who answers. The person who replies may be the person most directly involved in the problem, or it may be the most worried, or it may be the family spokesman. In any case, the therapist will obtain further information concerning the rules that govern the interactions between the members of the system.

---

lished pattern of negotiation." I have frequently found it useful to enter a temporary coalition with one of the family members, but only for a specific tactical purpose. In coalitions of this kind, the family member serves as temporary co-therapist.

Each family member will feel that he is expected to answer. Usually, if the problem concerns a young child, the mother will be the first to respond, talking about the history of the disturbance and possibly about what she sees as it's "causes." Sometimes the father adds to the description, elaborating on some aspect of the problem, or else he may merely implicitly confirm what his wife says. It rarely happens that an open question like this will stimulate differentiated replies from the parents and the identified patient. The identified patient, who feels that he is the source of family difficulties, usually thinks that the question is not really directed to him, and he doesn't feel entitled to express his own opinion about it.

The response will be different if the therapist questions the family members individually. For example, he can ask each one, "What do you think the problem is?" Then the answer will be more personal and more analytical. The diversity of replies will help the therapist to verify some of his suppositions concerning the relationship between personal autonomy and the interactive requirements of the system. Asking this kind of question guarantees each member's freedom to reply, thereby reinforcing the process of differentiation initiated earlier in the session.

To further this process of differentiation, the therapist's verbal and nonverbal interventions have to be consistent. For example, he can utilize space and physical contact by moving himself and shifting the center of attention from one family member to another, thereby preventing "induced" or evasive responses. This is particularly important with adolescents or younger children, who frequently say what their parents want them to say, rather than what they really think. The therapist can also put the question in another way, by asking each person, "What do you expect from this meeting?" By formulating the question that way, the therapist receives less ambiguous answers. His intention is to find out what the family's expectations are, rather than to learn specifically about the presenting problem. Or else he can ask, "What changes would you like to see in the family?" This question shifts attention from the disturbance to a consideration of possible transformations of the existing situation. The question has the advantage of emphasizing the possibility of constructive change and the group's desire to achieve it, without entering into the details of the problem. On the other hand, this question prematurely introduces the idea of change as a therapeutic goal in abstract, generic terms, before intrafamilial and extrafamilial relations have been explored. In fact, this is just what the family often hopes for when it starts therapy: to change things without changing anything in the *status quo*. [14]

Wrong and Right Ways of Gathering Information

If we analyze how the therapist proceeds in gathering information in this initial phase of therapy, we notice the profound difference between a systemic approach and a traditional approach. Many of the rules of behavior followed by a traditional therapist become major obstacles for an interactional therapist.

If a therapist wants to be consistent in using a systemic approach, then he must avoid doing certain things:

1. He must not make interpretations or comments to help a person to see the problem in a different way. For example, a young mother is very upset and thinks her 5-year-old daughter is "depraved" because she continually "touches herself." A traditional therapist would try to convince her that the matter is not as serious as she thinks, or he would point out that her reaction is out of proportion to the problem she is describing. Instead, in a systemic approach, the therapist accepts what she says and tries to "see" this information in interactional terms. He will probably ask further questions concerning the circumstances in which the behavior occurs, in order to clarify its interactional significance in the family system.

2. He must not give advice. If the therapist accepts the role of counselor, he eventually has no alternative but to intervene by supplying solutions to the problem from the outside (this would be particularly gratuitous at the beginning of therapy, when the therapist as yet knows nothing about the group's dynamics). Even when some family member requests advice or when a pressing problem seems to justify offering suggestions, if the therapist complies he will prevent the family from assuming responsibility for its past or determining its own transformation.

3. He must not allow himself to become involved in the emotional responses of family members to the problem. This doesn't mean that the therapist should not give consideration to what each member subjec-

---

[14]The therapist, as an agent of change, risks placing himself in an awkward position. In his efforts to modify the rules that support the system's homeostasis, he risks adopting a judgmental attitude. If this occurs, he finds himself in a symmetrical or disqualifying position vis-à-vis the family, and consequently his chances of joining the family system are greatly reduced.

tively experiences, but that at this time he should be more interested in gathering facts and opinions from each person.

Frequently, families with very serious difficulties and with recurring acting out on the part of the identified patient try to get the therapist emotionally involved in their difficulties by presenting their situation in a highly dramatic way. If the therapist allows himself to be overwhelmed by the emotional climate created by the family, he has little chance of establishing a therapeutic context. He is easily forced into a passive role, and he is manipulated by the family systems' homeostatic forces. Moreover, he will have no access to the constructive energies existing in the system.

This kind of risk is often present in outpatient settings or home visits with families in acute crisis. It is hard to calculate how many emergency hospitalizations (and consequent hospital "careers") could have been avoided if the therapist had managed to stay out of the emotional storm. If he maintains adequate "distance," a therapist can interrupt the vicious circle that is supporting the crisis by exposing the dysfunctional transactions in which the identified patient and the family system are locked. It is technically possible for a competent therapist to intervene effectively in this sense. But it is quite hopeless to expect a public psychiatric service to approach a crisis situation this way. In general, these services merely aim to bring the crisis under control, and the traditional psychiatric premises on which interventions are based usually lead to the stigmatization and isolation of the individual in crisis.

A few basic rules concerning how to gather information about a system's interactional patterns and how to activate change emerge from these observations:

1. Each family member should be encouraged to express his opinion about the problem, so that the therapist can observe each person's level of autonomy. In every family, there are some people who express themselves easily and who may even speak for other members who have more difficulty or who prefer not to commit themselves. At this point, the therapist begins to analyze the degree of differentiation attained by each member of the family as a system.[15] The therapist makes

---

[15]The concept of differentiation has been described by Murray Bowen (1966). According to Bowen, the degree of family pathology is proportional to the degree of differentiation of the family ego mass.

In Minuchin's (1974) structural approach, the gravity of the situation depends on the degree of permeability of personal and interpersonal boundaries within the family system.

use of space, of his own creativity, and of his therapeutic power for this analysis.

For example, in talking to a child, the therapist must do more than just elicit a reply. The therapist has to use the child's own language and accept his nonverbal responses; he must enter the child's world and speak to him while playing with him or sitting next to him. The therapist must prevent the parents from interfering with the child's responses by words or gaze. If the therapist wants to communicate with an elderly person, he should not expect abstract or very detailed replies that are far removed from the facts of the individual's daily existence. Nor should the therapist minimize or ignore any family experiences that the members consider relevant to an understanding of the problem.

When the problem concerns the marital relationship, the "normal" partner often tries to intrude into the personal territory of the "sick" partner. The former usually feels he has the right to define the other's feelings and thoughts, while systematically avoiding talking about his own. The therapist should test the rigidity of these mechanisms, encourage each partner to express his own ideas, and in general, try to delimit each partner's area of autonomy.

2. If someone interrupts another speaker, the therapist should take note of what the other speaker was saying and to whom he was talking when the interruption occurred, and he should prevent further interruptions. Sometimes the therapist can block an interruption easily by commenting on it verbally or by a simple hand gesture. In other cases, when the family rules prescribe that whatever one person says must be disqualified by another member, the therapist has to act as policeman. He has to use all of his resourcefulness to induce the participants to observe at least minimum rules of mutual respect. Otherwise, he finds himself involved in a hopeless situation.

He also has to prevent the family members from speaking for each other or using the term *we*, thereby giving only generic, noncommittal responses.

3. The therapist should encourage the members of the family to talk about their problem in concrete terms. He should refuse to accept abstract or generalized descriptions, such as, "He has turned inward and doesn't communicate with us anymore"; or "He has changed; he used to be part of the family, now it's as though he were no longer there"; or "My problem is that my parents don't understand me any more"; or "Our marriage is a complete failure."

The more concretely a problem is described, the easier it will be to elicit opinions about it and to formulate a therapeutic goal.

While the therapist is asking questions and encouraging the family members to speak, he simultaneously observes how each person behaves and notes what each person says, to determine whether or not behavior and verbal messages are congruent.

When one of the family members talks to the therapist, the therapist watches the reactions of the others. The other family members may openly or surreptitiously communicate hostility, boredom, agreement or disagreement, pleasure, or indifference.

Particular attention should be given to the responses of a child or an adolescent identified patient while the parents are talking about him. An interactional analysis of the child's attitude and his behavior in the session can provide a series of useful elements for a more complete understanding of the problem.

The therapist carefully observes the reactions of the father when the mother is speaking, and vice versa, because sooner or later he will probably have to deal with some area of conflict between them. Their conflict may be expressed through the child. In fact, it is almost a fixed rule that a disturbance in a child reflects problems between the parents.[16] The way that the parents present their child's problem[17] is therefore particularly important.

Activating the System

In this phase, the goals of the therapist are:

1. To activate direct communication between family members about the problem or other related questions. The therapist's position becomes less central.

2. To receive further information concerning the family's structure and its transactional rules. The therapist observes how the family members relate to each other; he gathers and selects the most important

---

[16]Vogel and Bell (1960) have extensively studied the ways in which a family member becomes a scapegoat. They have found that in all of the families studied, one child was drawn into a conflict between the parents. In disturbed families, the parents live in deep fear of the marital relationship and of their parental roles. They feel that they are unable to predict how their partner will respond to their behavior. Nonetheless the partners response is felt to be extremely important and potentially dangerous.

[17]For a discussion of listening to the metaphorical sense of communications, see the section in Chapter 4 titled "Metaphor as a Means of Communication," p. 137.

verbal and nonverbal information; he makes hypotheses concerning the functional and dysfunctional sequences that occur during the session.

3. To prepare the way for a definition of a therapeutic goal.

The following case material shows how this interactive phase of the session develops.

The Case of Sandro: Where Is the Epilepsy? [18]

Sandro is 12 years-old and has suffered from epileptic disturbances since the age of 4. Pharmacological treatment has successfully kept his illness under control to the extent that he has had no clinical manifestations for several years. He has been referred for a family consultation, after several brief periods of individual therapy, because of behavioral difficulties. His mother describes his behavior as tyrannical and overbearing, particularly in the last two years, during which he has begun to spend more time out of the house.

It is the mother who telephones the therapist. She says that she is exhausted and pessimistic about Sandro's incurable disease. She says that she feels unable to cope with him: he demands that she wash and dress him and prepare special meals for him, and he generally tyrannizes her.

She tells the therapist that a family consultation has been suggested by the neurologist who has been treating Sandro. Then she adds that she doesn't think her husband will be able to come to the interview and that, in fact, she herself is not very optimistic about the meeting. She repeats several times that epilepsy should not be discussed in front of Sandro, "because the child shouldn't know about it."[19]

[18]In families with a child who has an organic disturbance, a diagnosis and therapy centered exclusively on the patient provide reassurance. The family is reinforced in its belief that the child's illness is the source of all its difficulties, while the system itself is not considered except as having to endure the effects of the child's handicap. The child's autonomy is probably unnecessarily circumscribed and the problem is amplified beyond the characteristics of the disease itself. These results are due to cultural beliefs and to social prejudice concerning certain diseases (epilepsy, mental retardation, etc.) as well as to the needs of the family system to utilize the disturbance. Therefore, an intervention that concerns only the child makes his role as a "patient" official, confirms the belief that his illness is the source of all family problems, and leaves the social prejudices unchallenged. The child's organic disease serves as a well that collects all familial and extrafamilial tensions, and all of the family members utilize it according to their needs.

[19]The therapist should never become involved in keeping family secrets. He should not treat things that everyone knows about as "secrets." He must create an open and frank atmosphere from the beginning of therapy, avoiding any complicity. Such an atmos-

Despite the mother's doubts, the whole Valeri family comes to the first session: father, mother, Sandro, Piero (Sandro's 17-year-old brother), and a maternal aunt (who has lived with the family since she was widowed).

After about half an hour, the picture appears more complex than described by the mother on the telephone. The mother confirms what she had previously said, but now, in describing Sandro's tyrannical and independent behavior, she also seems to be proud of him. She uses his illness to justify his behavior.

The aunt adores Sandro and is quite willing to let him have whatever he wants. She sleeps in the same room with him "because he might have a crisis during the night" (this has never happened). Therefore, he cannot sleep alone, nor can he sleep with his brother because the two fight "like cats and dogs."

The mother describes Piero as patient, judicious, and mature. Sandro and Piero really do behave like cats and dogs. They watch each other hostilely and provoke each other repeatedly during the session. Positive relations between the siblings seem to be obstructed by their respective alliances with the aunt and the mother.

The father is a construction adviser and says that he is absorbed in his work at building sites. He seems to be a competent, down-to-earth person. This is the first time he has ever been personally involved in Sandro's therapy and seems to be very willing to cooperate. He claims that Sandro's only "illness" is that he is spoiled by his aunt and his mother. The father says that the mother continually complains about the boy's behavior but invariably supports him in everything. He adds that the aunt spoils Sandro and protects him because she considers him weaker than other children of his age. From the way the father expresses himself, it is clear that he is speaking not only about Sandro but about his wife and his sister-in-law and his relationship to both of them as well.

When the therapist asks Sandro's opinion on his father's comments, the boy seems to agree with his father. The fact that Sandro accepts a redefinition of his illness in interactional terms (being spoiled by his mother and aunt) is important, and it indicates a potential area for the therapist to work on. On the one hand, Sandro evidently uses cap-

---

phere prevents the family from hiding behind a façade and allows the therapist to enter into contact with the family's reality and needs. Otherwise the family system will successfully manipulate the therapist, who will lose his therapeutic power.

ricious behavior to tyrannize the family and obtain secondary advantages; on the other hand, he apparently wants to create a more age-appropriate identity for himself.

Formulated in interactional terms, the problem is no longer Sandro's epilepsy, which received no further mention in the rest of the therapy, nor is the problem Sandro's disturbing behavior (which had previously been seen in linear terms as the consequence of his illness). Sandro's inadequate behavior seems to be the result of a series of interpersonal interactions and conflicts between the adult members of the family as well as between the siblings.

Therefore, the principal scope of therapy is to offer the family an alternative, accepting the problem the family presents but changing or broadening its significance.

The following sequences are taken from the interactive phase of the first session:

THERAPIST (*to the father*): I have the impression that you have your own ideas about Sandro's problem. Do you think you can help me to get a better picture of the situation?

The therapist touches the father on the shoulder, reinforcing his request for help by a friendly gesture.

FATHER: Certainly, why not? If I can be helpful . . .

THERAPIST: Listen, Sandro has said that he agrees with your "diagnosis" that he is spoiled. That in itself is a positive thing, finding a father and son who agree about things.

By emphasizing the positive value of their agreement, the therapist reinforces the alliance that probably exists between father and son, before asking them to confront each other.

Now I would like you to talk to Sandro about this question of being spoiled, particularly about what it means in concrete terms in the family, and whether you can see some way of getting over it.

The therapist asks for more than a theoretical analysis of the situation. He now assigns them the task of seeking possible solutions.

THERAPIST (*to Sandro who is sitting between his aunt and his mother*): Why don't you move your chair over and sit facing your father? That way we (*to the other family members*) can listen without disturbing you.

The therapist wants to prevent the mother and the aunt, and perhaps the older brother as well, from interrupting. He also stresses the importance of listening, and he moves his own chair close to the other members who form the audience. This gives an "official" aspect to what is about to take place. [20]

SANDRO (*smiling*): Should I take my chair? (*He moves toward his father, while the therapist takes his place between the mother and the aunt*).

FATHER: Well, let's see where to begin (*with a friendly but serious tone*). First of all, I don't like all that fuss you make about eating. Your mother must really be at her wit's end because you don't want vegetables, you can't stand cheese, the meat is never cooked the way you like it. Isn't that true?

SANDRO: Yes, that's all true, but I'm not going to eat chicory, even if you kill me. . . .

FATHER: The second question is hygiene. You know what I mean! How come your mother has to wait on you hand and foot as though you were a baby?

---

[20]*Restructuring space* is a simple and effective way of exploring or activating relationships among the family members and provides information about the family's preferred transactional patterns. The use of space, an essential aspect of nonverbal communication, will be examined in Chapter 3. The therapist can manipulate space in therapy to release the self-therapeutic energies present in the family system, sometimes obtaining dramatic results.

MOTHER (*forcing her way into the conversation*): And if I don't run to him right away when he calls me from the bathroom (*speaking to the therapist*), he just sits on the "throne" and screams like a madman, as though I were his personal slave.

THERAPIST (*to the mother*): Why don't we let Sandro and Dad talk about it for the moment? I would like you to help me see how far Dad and Sandro can get when they talk things over like two adults.

The therapist tries to prevent the mother from intervening on this subject, in which she feels directly and resentfully involved. Her intervention is an attack on Sandro and represents an attempt to disqualify him as an adult. The mother is also trying to prevent the father-son dialogue from continuing.

SANDRO (*visibly irritated*): I've had enough, I want to leave.

FATHER (*giving Sandro a friendly tap on the knees*): Well, what are we going to do? Are you going to act up here, too? The doctor has asked us to talk like two grownups. Now what kind of impression are we going to make on him?

The father is now taking over the function of co-therapist and seems to be very effective with Sandro.

SANDRO: Go ahead, continue.

FATHER: Then there is also the question of money. Your mother gives you fifty cents a day besides money for breakfast. Why do you have to go and pester your aunt down at the store and fill your stomach with junk besides?

The father is giving new information about the other adults in the family. He would like to stop the aunt from interfering with Sandro's upbringing. He may also be alluding to interference by the aunt in his marital relationship, but this is not the right moment to explore this area.

SANDRO: Fifty cents a day isn't enough. Besides, Piero gets two dollars, on account of his motorcycle (*he glares at Piero*).

FATHER: We could talk it over with Mother and maybe raise it. But you will have to quit going to your aunt at the store.

THERAPIST (*to the father*): I can see that you really know what you want from Sandro. I am thinking of asking you and Sandro to negotiate on these things you have mentioned, drawing up a written contract that you both sign.
But first I would like you to talk to your wife and sister-in-law about those aspects that concern them too. If they don't collaborate, I don't know whether the contract will work? What do you think?

Sandro looks obviously pleased at the idea of signing a "contract" with his father.

Now the therapist stimulates father-mother and father-sister-in-law interaction so that he can also explore other familial relations.

FATHER (*to the wife*): Do you agree with me that Sandro has to stop acting like a baby? But you have to stop letting him have his way. He has to eat the same things that Piero eats; he has to keep himself clean by himself and stop complaining. Is that clear?

MOTHER (*offended*): I'll certainly be glad if Sandro grows up, but you will have to do something with him. If you're never home, I'm the one who has to put up with his nonsense. And I'm fed up with it. Is that clear? Your son talks back to me like a truck-driver. I can't imagine where he picked up that language. I don't dare ask him to do anything around the house—he won't even go to buy bread for me. If Piero wasn't there to give me a hand, I don't know how I'd manage (*looking proudly at Piero*).

AUNT (*in angelic tone of voice*): But Ada, you see, Piero is four years older than Sandro. You have to let the "little one" have what he needs.

The alliances between the mother and Piero and between the aunt and Sandro emerge. At this point, these alliances seem to serve in avoiding a direct confrontation between the two sisters.

PIERO (*out loud*): All Sandro needs are the chocolates and candies you give him all the time! Hah!

SANDRO: Look who's talking, the saint of the family. And what do you buy with the money you get every day?

THERAPIST (*to the father*): I'm losing track of things. What were you and your wife discussing?

The therapist has observed a series of interactions that help him to visualize some of the family coalitions. Now he wants to bring the discussion back to the original subject, because he wants the father and Sandro to confront each other on concrete issues.

FATHER (*to the wife*): From now on I will worry about Sandro. You just have to tell me about everything that he does in the house. But you have to stop giving in to him.

The father offers to take more responsibility, but only if his wife agrees to cooperate by not "spoiling" Sandro anymore.

MOTHER: I'll be more than happy if you decide to spend more time at home. I'll be delighted to turn the whole problem over to you.

FATHER (*to Sandro*): I am going to raise your allowance fifty cents a day. I think it's fair that you should have a few cents to spend for yourself, but only on condition that you stop bothering your aunt, and that Mom doesn't keep telling me that you have been driving her wild, the way you usually do.

FATHER (*to his sister-in-law*): Eleanora, you have to stop giving him candies and chocolate . . . besides, they ruin his stomach.

AUNT: I can't see what harm can come from a little milk chocolate now and then.

PIERO (*aloud*): Now and then! But Sandro is down at your drugstore all day long stuffing his mouth with chocolate and candies!

SANDRO (*to his brother, with anger*): You just mind your own business!

AUNT (*to the father*): Anyway, I don't want to have any more to do with it. You're his father, but I still don't think you should take him by the horns. He is more sensitive than other children.

The father has understood the therapist's suggestion about making a contract with Sandro, and is starting to list the clauses.

Is the aunt alluding to Sandro's epilepsy or to his need for protection by the adult members of the family? It seems that the aunt wants Sandro to remain a child in order to maintain her own role in the system. If Sandro matures and accepts independence, then the adults will inevitably have to deal with their own interpersonal problems.

We can now analyze some of the more important elements that emerge from the family's interactions during this part of the session.

The coalitions between the mother and Piero and between the aunt and Sandro have at least four pragmatic effects:

1. They interfere with the development of positive relations within the sibling subsystem. As a result, Piero and Sandro fight with each other, behaving according to their respective stereotyped roles of "the sick son" and "the normal son." Sandro's role is justified by his epilepsy.

2. They keep the father out of large areas of family life, relegating him to a peripheral position. He very likely behaves in a way that encourages the maintenance of family alliances that exclude him, so that the process is probably circular. Furthermore his absence from the house cannot be explained by the demands of his job. In the opening phase of the session, he had said that his work was demanding but that it left him ample free time to spend with friends and to go hunting over the weekends.

3. They prevent Sandro from achieving autonomy. (Piero's situation is different. He seems to be quite independent.) Sandro's organic disturbance may have been the pretext for blocking or at least retarding Sandro's progress toward age-appropriate autonomy.

4. Direct confrontation among the adult members of the family is avoided by scapegoating one of the children.

By encouraging father and son to establish a special relationship during the session, the therapist can evaluate to what extent the father can help Sandro to achieve greater autonomy. In interactional terms, Sandro cannot become more autonomous unless other changes in the family's interpersonal relationships occur at the same time. If the father spends more time at home, this will probably activate new interactional patterns; but it will not in itself provide an adequate basis for a marital union that can endure without the mediation of a scapegoat. In seeking new ways to help Sandro achieve greater autonomy, the therapist will explore the family's dynamics more fully, and he will try to modify the relationship between Piero and Sandro (Piero could help Sandro if the two brothers were not involved in alliances that tend to separate rather than unite them). And if the aunt has to give up the satisfactions she derives from protecting her "little boy," she will have to find another source of emotional gratification.

Here the assignment of a task during the session has produced a pragmatic definition of the therapeutic system. This definition clearly excludes any expectation that the therapist will offer ready-made solutions to the family's problem. The situation activated in the session has created the kind of redistribution of responsibility that is needed to formulate a therapeutic contract.

THE THERAPEUTIC CONTRACT

As we have seen, the earlier part of the session is devoted to gathering information about the family's transactional patterns. This information is needed in order to formulate a therapeutic contract, which constitutes the basic requirement for the creation and successful functioning of the therapeutic system.

The contract consists in the definition of a therapeutic goal. It also represents a commitment on the part of each family member to work toward the desired goal. This means that the therapist-family relationship has to be defined before a contract can be negotiated.

The amount of time necessary before a contract can be formulated is another indication of a system's rigidity. In more flexible systems, the therapeutic contract can often be defined in the first or at most in the second session.

In reality, the goal stipulated in the contract represents a hypothesis or a plan of work. The more concretely it is defined, the more effective therapy will be. If the goal is vague, the greater the possibility is that confusion and misunderstanding will arise during the course of therapy. Vague objectives are hard to attain. Furthermore, if the goal is clearly defined to begin with, it will be easier for the therapist to evaluate the success of therapy.

Clear objectives also reinforce the family's commitment to therapy. The therapist, by assigning tasks and analyzing the family's interactions in the sessions, creates a climate conducive to learning. He encourages the family to experiment with new ways of relating, which can then be tried out in the context of their everyday lives. In this way, therapy is extended beyond the confines of the session, and the family itself becomes the therapeutic setting. The sessions, in turn, become the context in which progress made by the family outside of the therapeutic system is verified.

One way of extending the family's perception of the therapeutic setting is to arrange a limited number of sessions. This will make all of the family members feel more responsible. In practice, it will act as a positive reinforcement for the therapist as well as the family. The family will have a clear idea of the duration of treatment and will be more able to evaluate the changes that occur.

Brief therapy is thought by some people to be superficial and incapable of producing lasting benefits. My own experience shows that this criticism is unjustified and that it fails to take into consideration the important part played by the family system in the therapeutic process. Criticism of this kind often reflects misunderstanding of the nature of an interactional approach. We do not intervene for the sole purpose of eliminating a symptom or relieving momentary distress. Intervention offers a sample experience, which in turn serves as a basis for further learning.

Mordecai Kaffman (1963) described this process as the snowball phenomena:

> The beginning of healthy changes in behavior and attitudes both on the part of the child and the parents induces further mutual shifts in the parent-child relationship with additional positive achievements. Therapy has served to break a vicious circle, and from then on clinical changes do not run parallel to the intensity of therapy.

Minuchin (1974) affirmed the same thing when he stated that "the family system has self-perpetuating properties. Therefore, the processes that the therapist initiates within the family will be maintained in his absence by the family's self-regulating mechanisms."

However, it is not always easy to formulate a therapeutic contract, nor is it always possible to plan a brief therapy. For example, particular problems exist in working with families characterized by schizophrenic transactions, where the members tend to disconfirm themselves and the others. The therapist has to resort to a series of maneuvers (without being disconfirmed himself) in order to join the family system. Difficulties also arise in working with the disengaged or enmeshed families described by Minuchin (1974). Minuchin's categories are based on opposed transactional styles, the disengaged families having diffuse boundaries and the enmeshed families having inappropriately rigid boundaries.

In each of these cases, the therapist has to deal with a rigid system. The basic requisite for formulating a contract is missing, because these systems cannot easily accept a therapeutic relationship in which the family is the protagonist of change and the therapist is a participant-observer. Rigid systems feel helpless and incapable of self-determination, and they invariably try to induce the therapist to become the protagonist of the therapeutic process. Furthermore, the rules of the system prevent the members from defining themselves in relation to each other or, therefore, to the therapist.

In fact, with a rigid system, a great deal of therapeutic work is needed before a contract can be formulated. The therapist has to open the system, creating new areas for interaction and encouraging greater confrontation among family members.

In therapy with rigid family systems, then, we cannot formulate a contract quickly without running serious risks. The family's definition of the therapeutic relationship is based on the delegation of all responsibility to the therapist and on the concept of individual mental illness. It is impossible, with these premises, to negotiate a contract with the objective of changing the rules of the system. The family expects the therapist to eliminate the disturbed (and disturbing) behavior by intervening at the level of the rules of the system. If the therapist attempts to negotiate in this situation, the resulting contract inevitably reflects the family's premises.

Generally speaking, the amount of time needed before a correct therapeutic contract can be reached with any family system depends on how accurately the therapist has gathered information in the preceding phases of therapy. The first session may not have provided enough information to enable the therapist to define a first goal. In this case, he arranges with the family to hold one or two more exploratory sessions, so that they can then review the situation together. The therapist must in all cases be able to identify the kind of difficulty that underlies the presenting problem. The disturbed behavior may be a signal of either intrasystemic or intersystemic difficulties.

Let's consider the example of a family composed of mother, father, and son in which the son is the identified patient. The family comes to therapy on its own initiative because of some kind of internal stress. The contract will probably be based on the presenting problem, that is, the problem of the son. Nonetheless, when the therapist asks the family to cooperate in seeking a solution to the son's difficulties, he implicitly requires them to clarify the real problem (which may be, for example, a marital problem). This means that although the contract is based on the presenting problem, it will not necessarily be limited to this problem. Once an exploration of the presenting problem has brought to light the transactional patterns of the family system, the objectives of the contract may be modified.

It may prove impossible to reformulate the contract, centering it on the real problem. For example, a couple may be unwilling to review the rules of their marital relationship. However, it is still important to make the couple realize that other ways of relating exist that do not depend on the utilization of a child.

The situation is different when a family comes to therapy on referral by a medical or an educational institution. The family is less motivated and can more easily deny its problems, or it can insist that these are due to some external factors. A family that comes in because it has been referred will probably try to defend itself from the therapist or else to seduce him (to form an alliance with him). The therapist is in danger of finding himself triangulated between two systems. To avoid this risk, the therapist must first assess several factors: (1) the pressure exerted by the referring agency on the family; (2) the probability that the family will accept therapy; and (3) the extent to which the behavior of the identified patient is indicative of difficulties existing between the family and the referring institution.

The therapist has to clarify the situation so that the family can free itself of any defensive or seductive attitudes or from any fear of being stigmatized. Once the context has been changed, the family may decide after ample consideration that it is sufficiently motivated to redefine its relationship to the referring institution. It may prove possible to work with the family in the institution or in family sessions in which representatives of the outside institution participate.

The following brief excerpt from a first session illustrates this kind of situation.

THERAPIST: Who would like to begin telling what the problem is?

MOTHER: Well, *the problem is that the school called* to tell me that Giorgio fights with his classmates and doesn't pay attention in class.

THERAPIST: Do you all agree?

MOTHER: Well, I don't go to school, so I can't really tell. It's true that his old teacher never complained. But now they tell me I should take him to a specialist! And maybe have an electroencephalogram!

THERAPIST: But how do you think he behaves at home, or with his friends?

MOTHER: He is very lively, that's true, but it seems to me that at his age, well, I think there are plenty of kids who are wilder than he is.

FATHER: But he has been more nervous lately, maybe with some tests. . . . You know how it is, we are a little worried that he might be abnormal in some way. If he doesn't have anything wrong after all this (*turns to the son*)—I'll really teach you a lesson!

Giorgio sulks with his head bowed during this part of the interview, without intervening.

"*The problem is that the school called.*" This brief phrase reveals the family's confusion. On the one hand, the family is worried that their son may have some real pathology; on the other hand, the family feels resentment toward a teacher whom they suspect may be incompetent and punitive with Giorgio.

The father intervenes only at the end and participates very little throughout the session. It later becomes clear that he feels completely extraneous to Giorgio's school life.

In this situation, the therapist proceeds on several levels.

1. He avoids letting Giorgio and the family formulate the problem in terms of pathology.

2. He denies that therapy is a psychiatric intervention intended to cure Giorgio's disturbance. In fact, the therapist denies that the problem exists *in* the family, and he directs the family's efforts outward to the extrafamilial source of the disturbance.

3. He formulates an agreement with the family to intervene on a different level. He offers to act, temporarily, as the mediator in a constructive relationship between family and school, after which he will withdraw from the situation.

4. Once a mechanism has been created to facilitate family-school relations, he invites the parents to maintain a clear relationship with the personnel of the school, and he encourages the father to take a more active interest in his son's scholastic activities.

In formulating a therapeutic contract, the therapist must also decide *where* to intervene. According to the particular case and circumstances, therapy may best be carried out in an outpatient setting, at home, at a school or other institution, or at times moving from one place to another as circumstances require.

A therapist may decide to hold sessions in the family's home for strategic reasons. For instance, he may want to see the family at home in a moment of crisis, or to assess a situation at the termination of therapy, or to visualize the relation between personal and interactive areas (particularly important in therapies with adolescents). Home visits should never become a routine practice. The therapist would inevitably interfere with the family's autonomy, thereby preventing a correct definition of the therapeutic relationship, in which the family is responsible for effecting change.

2

Redefinition in Family Therapy

One of the principal objectives of therapy is the relief of the state of suffering for which an intervention has been sought. But *suffering, psychiatric symptoms,* and *madness* take on different meanings according to the way we consider them. If we consider them *mental disturbances* inherent in individuals, we will inevitably study the nature of the patient and seek within him the causes of distress. Consequently, therapy will consist in the administration of drugs or of those physical or psychological treatments thought most appropriate to the particular case. But if the same signs of suffering are seen as a signal of a larger disturbance that affects and is in turn affected by other factors, then we will look for the interactional significance of the disturbed behavior and its implications for the family and the social context in which it has appeared. In this case, therapy will consist of helping the identified patient overcome his difficulties in a changed context whose own latent therapeutic capacity has been rediscovered and activated. In this altered context, the disturbance will no longer be experienced as a stigma but as an incentive to the growth of a group that shares a common history.

Therapy centered on the individual and delegation of responsibility to an expert are the cornerstones of the psychiatric approach based on the *medical model* of disease, which assumes that the object of therapy is a sick individual. This model is generally accepted by both mental health workers and the majority of persons who utilize their services in public as well as private facilities.

Clients and therapists have complementary roles and functions: the former are supposed to furnish information concerning the problem, whereas the latter are expected to identify the *causes* and to intervene accordingly.

It is easy to predict how a relationship of this kind—usually called *therapeutic*—will be defined: the patient expects to receive therapy—that is, the resolution of *his* problems—by an expert who is willing to treat him. In fact, the expert is expected to resolve the patient's problems for him, *by substituting for him*. If the patient does not harbor these expectations, either the family or an agent of some institution (a school, a medical center, etc.) will probably try to convince him that an intervention, which *they* have requested, will be useful to *him*. This procedure is almost invariably followed in the case of children and psychotics, who are too often deprived of self-determination. Therapy undertaken on this basis is inevitably ineffective and encourages passivity. It provides stereotyped responses to needs that are not fully understood and that are often quickly transformed into diagnostic labels.

The apparent conformity between the request of the client and the response of the mental health worker supplies the rationale for maintaining forms of treatment based on a rigid medical model of disease. It also perpetuates a *stereotype of the relationship between the people who have the power to cure, because they are sane, and the people who have the right to be treated, because they are sick.* As a result, the symptom becomes the object of the therapeutic relationship; it is classified and forced to conform to a rigid scheme; and it becomes increasingly irreversible. The therapist's modalities of soliciting and giving information, his attitudes, his ways of speaking and moving in the therapeutic sessions, the choice of intervention—these will all be influenced by the basic assumption that the person who demonstrates disturbed behavior is "sick." In this situation, every aspect of the intervention will take on a specific significance (Haley, 1975).

Even the space in which the encounter takes place is designed to emphasize the differences between the participants' roles and functions. Desk, couch, white coat, clinical record, prescription pad, and drugs help to establish a *safe distance* between the person who dispenses the service and the client, and to underline the distinction between the sane person and the sick one. This way of structuring therapeutic space reflects the conventional social image of mental illness in which "the image of madness is inversely symmetrical or complementary to the image of normality" (Jervis, 1975).

REDEFINITION OF THE THERAPEUTIC RELATIONSHIP

When we consider the therapeutic intervention from a systemic perspective, where the aim is to restore to the group in question the management of its interactional problems, we face a very different set of problems. How should we intervene, where, with whom, in response to which requests, and with what objectives? To answer these questions, we have to redefine therapy, *not as an intervention centered on a "sick" individual, but as an act of participation and growth in a group with a history:*

> If we adopt the systems approach, we can no longer be satisfied by a "psychiatric diagnosis" which perpetuates and crystallizes situations that are still capable of change. Instead, we explore the patient's interpersonal context as the primary means for developing adequate responses to symptomatic behavior. (Andolfi & Menghi, 1976a)

An effective therapeutic relationship is not created automatically, even when the therapist refuses to accept a delegation of responsibility and has shifted his interest from the *explanation* of individual behavior to the *observation* of family interactions. Usually the family's expectations are based on the psychiatric logic of delegation and of illness in individuals. Although this concept of mental illness frightens the family, it also provides reassurance: disease in an individual member explains the difficulties of the entire family (who must endure its effects), while the other members need not feel directly implicated.[1]

Therefore, the therapist's first task is to change the stereotyped expectations that the family brings into therapy. He must redefine the therapeutic relationship in a way that requires the family to assume responsibility for solving its interactional problems as these become clarified with the therapist's help.

Intervention can be radically transformed only if the therapist abandons the role of *deus ex machina* of the situation and if the family assumes active responsibility for the process of change. This means that the therapist must acquire a new form of *power*, based on his capacity to become actively involved in the contradictions, roles, and social stereotypes that weigh so heavily on the family and on the therapeutic team.

Only then will the family be able to try out new experiences. Often the family has long desired such experiences, but it has been paralyzed by fears that have been denied in order to maintain an appearance of "normality." In many cases, the therapeutic experience becomes for the couple, the children, or the extended family an opportunity for reflec-

---

[1]"The family's approach to their problem is usually oriented to the individual and to the past. The family is brought into therapy by the deviance or pain of one member, the identified patient. Its members' goal is for the therapist to change the identified patient. They want the therapist to change the situation without changing their preferred transactional patterns. In effect, the family is asking for a return to the situation as it was before the symptoms of the identified patient became unmanageable" (Minuchin, 1974).

tion and clarification—at times dramatic—concerning their methods of communication. These are often based on stereotyped patterns, hidden complicities, and rigid sexual and family roles, which prevent family members from achieving autonomy and bind the identified patient to the role of scapegoat.

The therapist's power is proportional to his capacity for self-questioning and his willingness to risk self-exposure. *"Therapy for the therapists"* is the way Jervis (1975) described situations where the therapist (and his group or therapeutic team) is called upon to explore and treat himself at the same time that he explores and treats the patient (together with his family, his colleagues, etc.).

In fact, the interactional therapist, freed from the concepts, methods, and terminology derived from the medical model, becomes an active and reactive part of the therapeutic system. The therapist's use of self transforms the therapeutic space into a field of dynamic interactions.

REDEFINITION OF THE CONTEXT

Therapy can be transformed to the extent that *the relationship between therapist and patient in the therapeutic situation is redefined.* This means that even the context—that is, the affective atmosphere and the physical space in which therapy takes place—must change. The context must allow the family to rediscover unexpressed areas and relationships so that the identified patient can abandon this role and the family can become its own therapist. Otherwise, "in the absence of a (contextual) frame of reference which is shared on at least a minimal level, misunderstanding and derailment of communication will inevitably occur" (Selvini, 1970).

What sense is there in asking a family to cooperate in the therapeutic process if drugs are prescribed to the identified patient (perhaps as a "precaution")? What is the purpose of encouraging new transactional patterns within the family system if the identified patient is confined in a mental hospital because he is "insane?" What are the limitations of an interactional intervention carried out by an isolated therapist in a clinic where policy is based on pharmacological control and maintenance of the *status quo*?

If a therapist tries to combine contrasting premises, there is a danger that he will create misunderstanding because of the discontinuity between the therapeutic situation and his redefinition of the relationship.

A viable context is essential if we hope to achieve satisfactory results in therapy. However, a satisfactory context is rarely formed without a process of redefinition. Our experience shows that the family brings into therapy its own network of interactional channels, its own definition of the presenting problem, and its own stereotyped expectations of therapy. In the initial phase of therapy, the context is usually defined on the basis of these elements: the more rigid and reductive these elements are, the more urgent and decisive the redefinition of the therapeutic situation should be. A description of some of the most common situations that we have observed may help in clarifying this concept.

We may speak of a *context of expectancy* to describe a situation seen frequently in which the whole attitude of the family rests on its expectation that a solution will be provided by the therapist. Expressions such as "Tell us what we can do in this situation"; "We have been sent to you for advice"; "We don't see why we should all be here, since the problem is our son"; or "We would like you to prescribe some shots for him" are frequently heard at the beginning of family therapy. Such comments are typical of the kind of reasoning that delegates to a specialist the task of changing whatever is wrong with the identified patient, or of instructing the family how to behave toward the "sick" member. The "sick" member himself, who expects to become the object of observation, usually asks nothing and assumes a passive, detached attitude.

It is usually easy to redefine this kind of context. To some extent, the family's expectations are based on the novelty of the therapeutic situation (with the whole family present). Understandably, the family expects the therapist to supply each member with an appropriate solution. Often it is precisely the newness of the family experience and the activation of all members, including the identified patient, that stimulate collaboration and make it possible to define a therapeutic objective in which the family becomes the protagonist of change.

Some families have a strongly blaming attitude toward the identified patient, whose "reprehensible" behavior threatens to undermine the family's social reputation. In these cases, we may witness the formation of a *judicial context,* in which the family more or less explicitly asks the therapist to make a judgment in favor of the parents, who feel threatened by the "abnormal" behavior of one of their children.

This situation creates greater difficulties for the therapist than the preceding one. He may unwittingly fall into a judgmental role, sentencing the identified patient; or he may assume a "protective" stance toward the patient, with the risk of increasing the family's guilt feelings and ultimately creating a courtroom situation. Or else he may attempt to avoid the problem with its surrounding tensions by concentrating attention on the relationship between the parents or on another child who does not present problems. In this way, too, he risks recreating a judicial context—this time with the parents in the role of the accused.

In these situations, the power of the therapist depends on his ability to break the vicious circle of guilt feelings without being trapped in it—and this is impossible without simultaneously *redefining the problem* for which the family has requested help.

An opposite situation exists in a *protective context*. Here the atmosphere is permeated by an aura of protectiveness and understanding of the behavior of a child. It makes little difference whether we are dealing with a child, an adolescent, or a young adult: he must be protected because he is fragile and "different." Protectiveness and passive acceptance of "disturbed" behavior are almost always present when a psychological disturbance appears in a person with some physical handicap or organic disturbance (epilepsy, retarded development, etc.).

A protective context is also frequently seen at the beginning of a couple's therapy, particularly in couples who appear very united and harmonious. Here the "sane" partner assumes a protective attitude toward the "sick" partner: the former claims to be in therapy exclusively because of his or her desire to help solve the partner's problem (depression, sexual difficulties, etc.). His or her wholehearted cooperation with the therapist in the initial phase is justified by a conviction that the sick partner cannot manage alone and must not be put under too much pressure. It is dangerous for the therapist to allow a protective circuit to persist in the sessions. If he, too, is drawn into the reasoning of "protect the person who is fragile," he will fail to grasp the interactional significance of the symptom and he will be unable to question the stereotypes that the couple has brought to therapy. Unless there is a clear redefinition of this kind of context, it will be hard for the therapist to maintain an impartial attitude or to prevent the formation of unconstructive alliances (often the partner who defines himself as "sane" claims a right to a privileged role in therapy). Furthermore it will be difficult to elicit a meaningful contribution from the identified patient if the therapist has agreed to consider him "immature" or "fragile" or in some way incapable of self-determination, *even* in the therapeutic situation.

Unquestionably the most difficult kind of situation to deal with is the *context of madness*. We are referring to situations characterized by a strong sense of unpredictability and impotence and by affective tones that tend to become intensely dramatic if a family member acts out a delirium or behaves in ways that appear manifestly abnormal. In these cases, apart from the objective difficulty of the situation, the family members will probably transmit to the therapist a message of implicit resignation, such as *"You see, he's really crazy, there's nothing you can do about it"*. Furthermore, the identified patient will probably confirm this judgment by the way he behaves.

Once a diagnosis of schizophrenia has been formulated and a "career" initiated in mental hospitals (that is, once the patient has been labeled as "different" with respect to the world of normality), an atmosphere of tension and inevitability may prevail in the sessions, even when the patient's behavior is entirely adequate or even when he is absent.

If the therapist accepts a "context of madness," he inevitably comes to experience the same feeling of impotence that has taken hold of the family members and the patient. His intervention will be ineffectual because it reinforces the family's feeling that it is faced with an irreversible process, with a chronic and degenerative disease. Paradoxically, the more ineffectual the intervention, the more massive becomes the tendency to delegate responsibility: the family demands a tranquilizing response to an insoluble problem. The therapist may seek an easy solution through therapeutic instruments such as hospitalization or drugs, which act "externally" without jeopardizing the delicate equilibrium of the family; above all, he may try to find a solution that does not expose him to his own irrationality or to the irrationality of others. The intervention becomes a *medical deception*, masking one of the biggest mystifications in psychiatry: the claim that an external agent can produce what the patient, his family and the larger community have failed to produce—that is, a change in the schizophrenic situation.

To redefine a context of madness, the therapist must first redefine his own parameters of normality.[2] He must immerse himself in a reality where normality and madness meet by discovering the *normality of the madness* of the patient. To succeed, he must feel free to express his own irrationality.

[2]"In reality, every 'mentally sane' person has mental disturbances, that is, psychiatric problems; and every person considered a 'psychiatric case' has psychological needs and problems which do not differ substantially from those of a 'sane person.' To invoke the presence of a disease to explain mental disturbances is to maintain that the dynamics of the disturbance are entirely different from those present in the normal psyche" (Jervis, 1975).

The therapist cannot enter into a family system long paralyzed by its particular perception of abnormality through the use of sophisticated techniques alone. He will succeed only if he negates his own diversity. If the therapist is able to enter the family system and the family is able to accept him, then madness is no longer a factor that creates distance, and it will lose much of its power. Therapy can then deal with a broader range of problems. We agree with Whitaker (1975) that therapy represents an opportunity for growth for both the family and the therapist:

> Therapy requires a different kind of participation by the therapist. Through his personal involvement and the rediscovery of the irrational parts of himself, he can demonstrate to the family the reversibility of the relationship normality-madness. In other words, the therapist demonstrates that madness is a role that can and should be played like any other role, but like other roles it must be reversible. (Anzilotti & Giacometti, 1977)

Redefinition of the Problem

Redefinition of the problem for which therapy has been requested is the cornerstone on which the entire therapeutic process rests. It is the most creative aspect of therapy and the one that makes it possible for the family to become the protagonist of its own change in the therapeutic situation.

For Watzlawick, Weakland, and Fisch (1974), the redefinition of the presenting problem is a modality of reframing, which means

> to change the conceptual and/or emotional setting or viewpoint in relation to which a situation is experienced and to place it in another frame which fits the "facts" of the same concrete situation equally well or even better, and thereby changes its entire meaning.

For these authors, as for Haley (1976), Whitaker (1975), Minuchin (1974), Bowen (1966), Hoffman (1971), Selvini *et al.* (1978), and other interactional therapists, the main goal of therapy is to increase the complexity of the situation rather than to restore order or to readapt the identified patient to a model of normality. According to their varying methodological bases, the means they use to obtain this goal and their use of the therapeutic context to encourage new individual and interpersonal experiences differ. Therefore, a therapeutic relationship and context that encourage an *a priori* and reductive definition of the problem must be modified from the outset:

> By considering the psychiatric intervention in a different light, it is possible to resolve difficult situations not by stigmatization or confinement, but by freeing

the individual from his role as scapegoat and the family from its role as culprit, thus permitting the family to discover its own self-therapeutic capacities. (Andolfi & Menghi, 1976a)

Redefining the Problem in Positive Terms

In a systemic approach, the problem is no longer seen as synonymous with a mental disturbance inherent in an individual but as an interactional node of familial and extrafamilial tensions. Therefore, to redefine the problem in positive terms, we have to change a conception of illness that is deeply rooted in each of the persons involved. A positive redefinition eliminates the *reductive* and *disparaging* aspects of the family's view of the disturbance. Once the disturbed behavior is seen in its interactional context, then the disturbance itself becomes a stimulus to seek new ways of relating.

Restructuring an experience felt by the family to be a stigma is a fascinating and challenging task. To succeed, the therapist has to alter the family's perception of mental disturbance as an individual attribute and thereby gain full access to the family system. With this objective in mind, he must avoid either a protective attitude toward the identified patient or an accusatory or commiserating attitude toward the other members of the family (respectively, the cause and the victims of a state of distress). The family's difficulties should not be minimized. The therapist should look for positive aspects that can help to transform the family's way of experiencing these difficulties.

Erickson, in his experience with hypnosis, observes that it is possible to "reframe whatever a subject does (or does not do) as a success and as evidence that his trance is deepening" (Watzlawick *et al.*, 1974). In this way, Erickson produces change by giving a positive connotation to every action. His strategy is based on the conviction that every person has a natural desire for growth and will cooperate if the positive aspects of his behavior are stressed (Haley, 1973).

In family therapy, a positive connotation is given to the interactional network that ties the members of the system to each other and to the therapist, and not to individual behavior. On this point, Selvini *et al.* (1978) call attention to the danger of falling back into a linear, causal model and assigning a positive connotation to the identified patient's symptom and a negative connotation to the symptomatic behaviors of the other family members. This would draw a line of demarcation be-

tween the components of the system, arbitrarily dividing them into good
and bad, and *ipso facto* precluding access to the family as a systemic unit.
It is also important to note that in assigning a positive connotation, and
in redefining in general, the therapist *challenges the meanings* that the
identified patient, the family members, the mental health professionals,
and the larger community have assigned to a given behavior over a
period of time, and that have made the behavior increasingly necessary
to the maintenance of the system's equilibrium and consequently more
irreversible.

The following example illustrates what I have said about redefining
the problem. Mr. and Mrs. Rossi request joint therapy after Margherita,
the wife, has had a lengthy individual treatment that has enabled her to
explore her conflicts but has not produced any significant change in her
self-destructive behavior. Margherita's face is covered with sores and
scars caused by scratching herself with her fingernails. She is a college
graduate, but she has never sought work. She devotes many hours a
day to her task of self-mutilation (taking great care to avoid infections).
Luigi, her husband, is a successful professional who is deeply involved
in a demanding job. He says that he has tried everything he can think of
to prevent his wife's self-destructive behavior, but without success. The
Rossis have an 11-year-old daughter who is clearly involved in her parents' problems. The following are a few sequences from the beginning of
the first session, in which the therapists (my wife was co-therapist) *challenge* the definition of illness presented by the parental system. They
attempt to redefine the problem in positive terms and to establish a
therapeutic context in which both partners can feel that they are the
protagonists of the process of change.

A little over 10 minutes have elapsed, during which Margherita has
given information about herself, using rather pretentious language. She
has described herself as a poorly defined person who has always been
forced into a dull and conventional role. She contrasts herself to her
husband, whom she sees as self-assured and satisfied with his social
standing.

MARGHERITA: You can see the   *Margherita presents herself as the iden-*
most obvious fact, just look at my   *tified patient and tries to impress the*
face. The problem arose when I   *therapists by a vivid description of her*
had my first relationship with a   *problems.*
man, that is, when I was intro-

duced to sex and to the demands of adult life. Then there was this explosion of a *neurotic symptom*, expressed by wrecking my face, to avoid using a cruder word for it.

THERAPIST: This is the first *creative* product of your curriculum vitae! It seems that in this sea of conformity the only creative thing you see or feel is what you have written on your face.

The therapist challenges the symptomatic behavior, redefining it in positive terms.

Where does the need to see the thing in neurotic terms come from?

The question is intended to raise doubts about the utility of labeling the problem and to undermine the power inherent in being "sick."

MARGHERITA: The question was pretty vague in the beginning. I felt that something was wrong. My face was the decisive factor . . . it was this symptom that began to spread terribly that made *us* understand why . . .

CO-THERAPIST: When you say that it spread, do you mean to your body, too?

The co-therapist reinforces the challenge by implicitly communicating that the therapists are not impressed, that in fact they expected something worse.

LUIGI: Only her face!

Now both partners reassure the therapists that the problem is not really as serious as they may think.

MARGHERITA: Only my face!

THERAPIST: The thing that strikes me the most is that you call it a *symptom*.

The intervention is reinforcing.

MARGHERITA: I say "symptom" in the sense of a terminal expression of something, like fever is to a disease. "Symptom" as an explicit, concrete manifestation . . .

LUIGI: You should explain that it's a symptom you create with your own hands. Anyone who doesn't know you might think it was something endogenous.

Luigi has apparently felt a challenge to the system and tries to bring the discussion back to the gravity of the self-produced symptom and therefore to the gravity of Margherita's condition.

MARGHERITA (*a little resentfully*): That seems quite superfluous to me.

THERAPIST (*to Margherita*): I don't think we're going to be able to start therapy by saying that you have a neurotic symptom, and that's all there is to it. You describe your life as extremely drab and conventional. But after all, you are free to live as you like. I don't see why you have to be such a conformist and call the only creative aspect of your life "neurotic."

By redefining the symptom as creative and describing it as the only creative area in Margherita's life, the therapist is implicitly challenging her to rediscover other areas of creativity that will permit her to feel less drab and conventional.

MARGHERITA (*with strong feelings*): Listen, what upsets me is that it is a destructive fact that becomes creative. I understand exactly the connotation you want to give to this expression of my individuality . . .

The therapist's provocation seems to be working; it is becoming more difficult for Margherita to insist on her "incurable symptom." A loss of control in this area may signify an acquisition of control in other more constructive areas.

LUIGI (*to Margherita*): We have to find out how all this works, because I have the impression that you can't explain exactly why this

Luigi fears a threat to the equilibrium of the system if the problem is redefined in positive terms. He returns to his original position.

happens to you. For someone who doesn't know you (*speaking to the therapist*), these aren't things that just happen by themselves, she does it herself with her own nails, that's the point!

THERAPIST (*unimpressed*): You already told me that on the phone.

MARGHERITA: I think that is all superfluous: it's perfectly clear that I do it myself.

THERAPIST (*to both*): That's where the creativity lies, because if it depended on, I don't know—say, on a problem of hormones—then it would really be a handicap. Not only that, but you carefully select the area, with a kind of symmetry . . . with a kind of creativity. (*To Luigi*) How often have you felt disgusted by the situation and wanted to give up and get a separation from your wife?

The therapist responds to Luigi's clarifications by insisting again on the theme of creativity.

At the same time, he lays the groundwork for releasing the husband from his "humanitarian" role.

LUIGI: Often, very often. At times it has been almost my only desire. What stopped me was my inability to make the decision, my *humanitarian feelings*. I don't really have any negative feelings toward Margherita—if it weren't for her illness, which in my opinion has caused our absurd relationship.

Is the illness the cause of their absurd relationship, or does it serve as an alibi for their failure to deal with their real problems?

THERAPIST: But if this is a part of your wife's life, a form of creativ-

If Margherita's self-destructiveness is a sign of creativity, there is no longer any

ity, of self-expression, why on earth do you feel so obliged to keep up a humanitarian attitude? You could easily make another life for youself.

CO-THERAPIST (*to Margherita*): How often have *you* thought of leaving your husband?

MARGHERITA: That is a very important question! I have a great deal of ambivalence about it. A separation from my husband would mean many things. Facing life alone. Being afraid of growing up, of living an adult role. I boycott myself with this symptom of mine, I'm looking for an alibi. . . . I'm satisfied with my husband, I've always gotten along with him in every way. We'll talk about the sexual problem later, because there are grounds there for the development of my neurosis. In marital matters, there is nothing that divides us, but as a couple, things don't work because the focalization of the problem is *in me* and *on my shoulders*. But I think he's got some problems, too.

reason for Luigi to feel tied to her because she is sick, and he can give up his humanitarian role. On the other hand, the therapist's message clearly contains a paradox: if Margherita is not sick, then, according to what Luigi has said, the marriage should be going well.

The co-therapist's intervention reinforces the therapist's refusal to accept that Margherita is sick and implicitly supports her potentialities. Even a woman who disfigures her face is capable of autonomous initiative.

Margherita feels supported and begins to talk about herself in a different way. It will be possible to initiate an interactional therapy once the context and the problem have been clearly redefined. The subject of separation allows the therapist to explore both partners' capacity for autonomy; specifically, their potential for working out a new definition of their relationship that will be healthier and more gratifying for both, either within the marriage or outside of it.

Amplification of the Problem

Another way of facilitating redefinition of the problem is to sharpen the family's perception of it in the sessions. The therapeutic space can be used as a sort of sounding board for the conflicts, expectations, and interpersonal tensions that have previously been unrecognized or concealed behind a façade of pathology in one of the family members. Anorectic symptoms, delusional behavior, depressive states, immaturity—these are some of the *targets* on which energies present in a family system converge, when a family strives to defend its rigid structure from threats to its equilibrium. By amplifying the interactional significance of the problem, we can make breaches in this inflexible structure and allow members to try out new transactional patterns.

One effective way of interrupting dysfunctional and unproductive transactions is to *dramatize* them in the sessions. We can activate the same rules about relating that have gotten the family stuck in a state of seemingly irreversible difficulty.

If the interactional patterns of the family are uncovered and made visible to everyone, it is harder for the family *to maintain the illusion* that all of its difficulties stem from the problem of one individual, and it is easier to produce change in the group. New processes experienced by the family in therapy are maintained outside of the therapeutic context by means of the family's self-regulating mechanisms.

Redefinition, then, does *not call attention to* something: it *teaches a new game*, thus making the old one seem useless (Wittgenstein, 1956).

The following case can serve as an example. The De Angeli family came to us after a long journey throughout Italy in search of a solution to the difficulties of their 12-year-old daughter, Laura. After consulting their hometown general practitioner, they had gone to a psychologist in Modena and then to a private clinic in Milan. Their efforts had brought about a crystallization of the problem, because the family had been looking for a person capable of providing a partial, temporary solution rather than a *real* comprehension of the family's interactional dynamics.

The following summary of what the parents reported during the first session is particularly revealing: "Laura wasn't feeling well. She was losing weight and she was very nervous. She was being treated by our local pediatrician who prescribed liver extracts, vitamin B12, and other medicines to keep up her strength. But she kept on getting thinner and more depressed. So the pediatrician advised us to go to a psychologist in Modena. She tested Laura and advised us to send the child away from the rest of the family, because the tests showed that Laura had a conflict with her mother and her younger sister, Marina. So, since we have relatives in Milan, I [*it is the father who is speaking*] took Laura and her grandmother there. Her grandmother came along because Laura said she loved her very much, and the doctor thought that she would be the best person to be with Laura. But [*adds the mother*] after spending a month with her grandmother, Laura changed her opinion about her. . . . [*The father continues*]: So we stayed in Milan for a month. We went to another specialist who diagnosed depression with secondary elements of anorexia. He prescribed other medicines and recommended that we hospitalize the girl together with her grandmother for a short period of observation. At that point, we opposed hospitalization—and here we are. Now we have come to you."

This futile and damaging series of interventions will probably continue unless the therapist rapidly redefines his own role, the therapeutic context, and the problem. He will have to oppose further manipulatory efforts in order to make the family reassume responsibility for its own interactional difficulties. Only by direct confrontation and by redistribution of roles, relations, and generational boundaries within the family will it be possible to banish the *phantom* of a scapegoat and to foster a process of mutual growth.

THERAPIST: Was your grandmother here the last time too?

The therapist had been observing from behind a one-way mirror while the family was replying to requests for information.

LAURA: Yes.

THERAPIST: Does your grandmother live with you?

FATHER: No, she lives in a nearby town, about six miles from us.

THERAPIST: She is the mother of . . . ?

MOTHER: My mother.

THERAPIST: She is still a young woman.

MOTHER: Fairly young.

THERAPIST: Is she an energetic person?

While the therapist asks about the grandmother, he is gathering information about the entire family, and particularly about the relationships between the father, the mother, and Laura.

LAURA (*whispering*): Very.

THERAPIST: What did you say?

LAURA: Very.

THERAPIST: Very energetic, eh?

MOTHER: She comes over to our house often, very often.

THERAPIST: For example, once a month?

LAURA: No, no.

MOTHER: Since we live very close to each other, she comes every time it comes to her mind.

THERAPIST: And how does she get there?

LAURA: By car.

THERAPIST: Does she drive?

LAURA (*seemingly irritated*): Yes.

THERAPIST: You have a very sportive grandmother. (*To Laura*) But you don't like these visits of your grandmother, do you?

LAURA: It's not so much her visits—it's her!

THERAPIST: Oh!

LAURA: It's her!

THERAPIST (*to Laura*): When your grandmother comes, what does she do? Does she get angry at you?

LAURA: No, not when we're all together, no.

THERAPIST: I don't understand. When I saw her from behind the mirror, she was very sweet!

LAURA: No, she only seemed to be.

THERAPIST: She seemed sweet. (*To the mother*): What do you think?

While directing attention to the grandmother, the therapist is beginning to get an idea of the power positions in the family.

MOTHER: Well, she's pretty bossy.

THERAPIST: Do you take after your mother?

MOTHER: Maybe.

THERAPIST: What do you think?

MOTHER: Yes, I think I really do.

THERAPIST (*to the father*): And what do you think about that?

FATHER: In some ways, yes, in others, no. Laura, what do you think? (*He addresses the question to his daughter as though asking for confirmation.*)

Both parents must ask Laura for confirmation before answering. This pattern will be repeated many times during the sessions.

MOTHER (*to Laura*): Can I tell the doctor that before you got sick, you were very close to your grandmother?

LAURA: Yes, yes.

THERAPIST (*to the mother*): Excuse me, do you always ask your daughter's permission when you want to say what you think?

MOTHER: Before, I never asked anyone's permission. Now, since we have this situation at home, for fear of hurting her feelings. . . .

LAURA (*interrupting*): Anyway, you have already told him!

MOTHER: . . . I ask her permission.

THERAPIST: Do you ask anyone else's permission when you want to express your opinion about something?

MOTHER: No one else's, *not* my husband's.

LAURA: No, now you ask everyone.

Laura controls all of the transactions and seems to have the function of family switchboard.

MOTHER: Maybe now I do ask everyone for permission because I feel a little like the person who's incriminated—if you know what I mean.

THERAPIST: You feel like that?

MOTHER: Yes, that's how I feel. I think twice before I open my mouth because I always think I'm making a mistake.

THERAPIST: That's a bad position you're in. (*To the father*): Does Dad ask Laura's permission too, when he wants to say something?

Now the therapist draws in the father in order to verify the distribution of power in the family and the generational boundaries.

FATHER: Not normally, not even now. Maybe I make mistakes sometimes, but I say what I think (*To Laura*): Isn't that true?

THERAPIST (*to the wife*): You know, it seems to me that your husband is imitating you very well!

The therapist exasperates the problem of control of the relationships: Laura's power is proportional to her parents' need to delegate it to her. Laura's position seems indispensable to her parents' relationship.

MOTHER: You mean my husband imitates me?

THERAPIST: In asking permission, he does just what you do.

MOTHER: It depends on how you look at it.

THERAPIST (*to Laura*): Move your chair over here, just halfway between Mom and Dad. (*Laura moves over and sits down between her parents.*)

By restructuring the therapeutic space, the therapist visualizes the relationships between the three. This emphasizes Laura's problem and her role in the maintenance of the parental subsystem.

MOTHER: Well, at the moment I think he really does!

THERAPIST (*to Laura, in a serious tone of voice*): Laura, are you a 12-year-old girl or King Kong?

The therapist challenges the system through its spokesman, Laura. At the same time he enables Laura to foresee the possibility of returning to the sibling subsystem.

LAURA: A 12-year-old girl.

THERAPIST (*to Laura*): Then why do they treat you at home as though you were King Kong? Do you know who King Kong is?

The therapist reinforces the provocation by insinuating that perhaps the parents need a "King Kong" daughter.

LAURA: Yes, sure.

THERAPIST (*to the younger sisters*): Do you know who King Kong is? (*Replying to their negative gestures*): All right, Laura—you explain it to them.

The therapist encourages Laura to demonstrate her competence in comparison to that of her sisters, using the theme of his provocation.

LAURA: He's a great big, strong ape; they even made a movie about him.

THERAPIST (*leaves the room and returns with a pile of cushions, which he puts on Laura's chair to raise her up higher. She is now in a position between her parents, and above them*): You see, I don't mean that you are like a great big ape, but that you are like a very big person who is higher than everyone else and whom everyone is afraid of. Have you noticed how Mom and Dad watch you when you speak? Say, how did you do it? When I was 12 I wasn't as important in my home as you are. Tell me your secret—how did you become so important?

LAURA (*from her elevated position, angrily*): I'm not important even now, I'm just normal.

THERAPIST (*to Laura*): Do your Mom and Dad ask permission more often from you or from your grandmother?

Once again the therapist challenges and ridicules Laura's parental role by comparing her to the grandmother.

LAURA: Permission? I don't think they ask either of us.

THERAPIST: What? Haven't you heard your mother say that she is afraid of making a mistake every time she opens her mouth and that she always feels embarrased?

LAURA: I don't believe it

THERAPIST (*to the mother*): You see, it's not just that you feel in a difficult position—people don't even believe you!

MOTHER: That's exactly the way things are.

THERAPIST (*to the father*): Do you believe that your wife has been in difficulty lately?

FATHER: Yes, I think she really has.

LAURA (*with a resentful tone*): Hm, hm.

THERAPIST: I have read your records, but frankly I would like you to help me understand what it is that we can work on together, because the matter is still not clear to me.

After the therapist has redefined the context and dramatized Laura's functional role in the family system, he asks the members to help him find a therapeutic goal. Once the problem has been amplified in this manner, it should be easy to initiate interactional therapy instead of working on the false problem of Laura's illness.

Laura remained seated on her pile of cushions, between her parents, for the entire session. The metaphor of King Kong recurred many times during the course of therapy—until there was no longer any need for King Kong, because the system was changing.

3

Space and Action in Family Therapy

NONVERBAL COMMUNICATION

Communication is essential to human life and social relations. But often, when we speak about communication, we automatically think of language. In fact, for a long time in many fields of study, verbal expression was considered the only important modality of communication

In recent decades, however, much research has been done on those modes of behavior that constitute nonverbal communication and on the relationships between nonverbal communication and spoken language.

According to Watzlawick, Beavin, and Jackson (1967), "if it is accepted that all behavior in an interactional situation has message value, i.e., is communication, it follows that no matter how one may try, one cannot *not* communicate."

As a consequence, each of us, through daily experience, learns to interpret the messages transmitted by the people with whom we interact. For communication to occur, there must be a transmitter, a receiver, and a message. The message is composed of a *content*, which is usually expressed by language, and a *form*, which is expressed in a nonverbal modality and which provides information concerning the relationship between the communicants and concerning the context.

Analogic or nonverbal communication includes body movement (kinesics): touch, gesticulation, facial expression, direction of glance; tone of voice; and sequence, rhythm, and cadence of words, as well as personal and interpersonal spacing. Philogenetically, nonverbal communication is very primitive. It can be observed in animals and in early

71

phases of human development. Some forms of nonverbal communication are universal and belong to the category of neurophysiological reflexes.

Ekman, Sorenson, and Friesen (1969), in a research study carried out in New Guinea, Borneo, the United States, Brazil, and Japan, have demonstrated that certain gestures and facial expressions are universally interpreted in the same way.

If we listen to a radio broadcast or a tape recording of a speech by a person speaking a language we don't know, we are unable to understand anything. But if we can see the person while he is speaking, we are able to deduce a certain amount of information from his facial expressions, gestures, etc., which invariably accompany speech.

Such observations confirm the hypothesis that nonverbal models of communication are not purely imitative and culturally determined by a specific social context, but that they also retain strong instinctive components that enable them to function as universally recognized signals.

In the behavioral sciences, there are two different ways of interpreting nonverbal communication:

In the *psychological approach*, nonverbal communication is considered an expression of emotions, a way of presenting the self. For example, a particular facial expression is believed to indicate a state of depression; another expression a state of well-being. In this manner, people are thought to *indicate* their personality by nonverbal modalities.

In the *communicational approach* (utilized particularly by anthropologists and ethnologists), posture, physical contact, and movement are studied in relation to their social context, that is, to the rules that regulate relationships within the group. If this approach is used, the observation of a family sitting together provides an incredible amount of information merely by the way in which its members move their arms and legs. If the mother crosses her legs first and then the rest of the family crosses their legs, repeating the same action, the mother is probably the person who initiates family interactions, even though neither she nor the rest of the family are aware of it. Her words may even deny that she is the leader. She may, for example, turn to her husband or children to ask for their advice.

Actually, these two points of view are not mutually exclusive, since human behavior can be simultaneously expressive and communicational.

In fact,

if the observer focuses on one member of a group and considers only the thoughts and intentions of that person, he will interpret his behavior as expressive. If he observes the same behavior in terms of the effects it "produces" in the group as a whole, then he has introduced a communicational point of view. (Scheflen, 1972)

The distinction between verbal and nonverbal modalities is very important in the pragmatics of human communication. These modalities differ fundamentally in:

1. *Their relationship to the object referred to by the communication*. The relationship between a word and the object it denominates is arbitrary and conventional. Conversely, an analogic communication has a direct and immediately intelligible relationship to the object it seeks to define. This difference between verbal and analogic modalities is particularly evident in therapy when the therapist gathers information about the family's history and the relationships among its members. It is often difficult, and at times dull, to talk about facts and emotions or to describe the relationships existing in one's own family group. But the results are usually extremely vivid and comprehensible when the same information is acted out without the use of verbal communication.

2. *Their capacity to transmit information about objects*. Information about objects is transmitted verbally, by the use of concepts. The transmission of culture relies principally on verbal communication. This is also generally true of the report aspect of any message. Analogic communication, on the other hand, is more useful and significant in communicating about relationships.

3. *Clarity or ambiguity*. Verbal communication is based on a yes/no principle. It conveys information that may or may not be understood according to the syntax of the language. Information is conveyed only symbolically (for example, communicating in words one's needs, desires, and emotions). Analogic communication, apart from its instinctive aspect, conveys information that may be understood in different ways by different people in different cultures (think of the different sensations evoked by a single analogic behavior such as a hug, a laugh, a hand shake). It is difficult to interpret analogic behavior because it lacks the properties that specify which of several possible interpretations is correct; nor does it have properties that distinguish among past, present, and future. It does, however, possess a semantic structure adequate to define relationships.

4. *Prevalence in particular subcultures and age groups*. Many studies,

including those by Minuchin, Montalvo, Guerney, Rosman, and Shumer (1967) and Bernstein (1960), confirm the hypothesis that verbal communication is used relatively more by the middle and upper-middle classes.

A person's preference for verbal or nonverbal modalities seems to depend above all on the culture to which he belongs. In working with Latin, Anglo-Saxon, and black families, I have observed the differing use and significance of words with respect to analogic modalities of communication. This kind of observation can be generalized (for example, to include social groups in the same country having diverse histori-cal and cultural traditions and dialects). Therapeutic interventions can fail to achieve their goals if the therapist has not learned the "grammar" of the group's nonverbal language and its relationship to the group's spoken language. The therapist learns about these aspects of a group's communicational style by living and participating in the social context in which language and behavior arise and take on their particular signifi-cance.

With regard to age groups, analogic modalities predominate in childhood and preadolescence, the phases in which play and fantasy constitute the richest and most spontaneous media for communication.

Incongruence between Form and Content

Once we have defined the context in which a given interaction oc-curs, we find that nonverbal language may either contradict or confirm verbal communication. The French saying, "c'est le ton qui fait la musique," may seem banal, yet the experience it describes is common to all of us. For example, a reprimand or an unpleasant comment have a different effect according to the tone, attitude, and expression of the speaker. Similarly, we can demonstrate in a variety of ways that we are not interested in a particular person, even though we may answer him politely.

When situations of this type occur in a therapeutic context rather than in our everyday life, the relationship between verbal and nonverbal communication (the congruence or incongruence between form and content) becomes extremely important.

The following is a brief communicational sequence from a therapeu-tic session with a family composed of the parents and an only son, Alfio, who is 8 years old.

To gather information about the problem, the therapist asks the parents to enumerate Alfio's "misdeeds" (the mother's term) and to list them on the blackboard. The blackboard is soon covered with a long list: Alfio throws lighted matches into the gas tanks of motorcycles; he has thrown a little girl into the fish pond; he has broken a very expensive vase at home; he has tried to burn down the house by setting fire to a chair; he steals comic books from the newsstand, etc. The therapist is struck, above all, by the way the mother and the father comment nonverbally on their son's behavior. Their attitude of satisfaction and complicity is in marked contrast with the sense of bewilderment and impotence that they express verbally.

Their complicity becomes even more evident when the husband asks his wife to show the therapist the results of Alfio's latest act of bravado: the purchase of five knives. The mother takes the evidence out of her handbag, showing the opened knives to the therapist. She then deposits them on the carpet of the therapy room, as though implicitly inviting the child to take action. In fact, while the parents are talking to the therapist about this "rash" purchase, Alfio takes the knives and starts to cut into the carpet. The parents make no effort to prevent him.

If the therapist does nothing but analyze the contents of what the mother has written on the blackboard or what she has said about Alfio, he would reduce the problem to an analysis of the child's inadequate behavior. He would lose sight of the interactional significance of the sequence as a whole and of the incongruence between the verbal and the nonverbal communications presented in the session.

In general terms, whenever people communicate with each other, they transmit information about a content and also about their relationship. Therefore, every communication affirms something about the relationship between the person who transmits the message and the person who receives it.

If the verbal contents of messages were always commented on congruously, every relationship would be clearly defined. But in reality, people often make affirmations that define a relationship in a certain way, while simultaneously contradicting this definition by another behavior that denies it. But no one can avoid communicating and defining himself in a relationship. When a person is offered two contrasting definitions and is obliged to reply, he can signal that his response is involuntary. Symptoms originate in this way. The advantage of symptomatic behavior is that it enables the person who manifests it to avoid defining himself in the way requested, by proposing a new definition of "involuntariness." In general, the healthier an interaction is, the more closely the relationship level is related to the content level. The more an interaction is disturbed, the greater the tension created by continual efforts to define the relationship, while the content level becomes less and less important.

THE MEANING OF SPACE

The utilization of space is a particularly fascinating aspect of human communication. In studying communicational behavior, we observe the individual's reactions in relation to his immediate spatial context, and we analyze the ways in which he uses space to communicate inner states and signals to other human beings.

Space is more than a series of geometric relationships. It is an expression of our essential mode of being. Every action involves both a change in our personal bodily space within the surrounding space and a progressive definition of our inner world, in the same way that the process of forging an identity involves a progressive differentiation and demarcation of inner and outer space.

Space is an innate and universal dimension of man's expressive and social behavior. Space defines the individual's territory, a place of his own, where he can find himself and at the same time negotiate relationships with others.

Psychoanalysis and psychodynamic therapies in general use the spoken word as their principal therapeutic instrument and means for understanding inner states. For example, free associations are used to penetrate the client's inner world. Emphasis is placed on talking about the patient's feelings and conflicts, which are then interpreted on the basis of his history and past traumas.

In interactional therapy, physical contact, movement, action, and the presence of others simultaneously produce associations, meanings, and behavior within the given context. Emphasis is placed on enacting and dramatizing emotional states and conflicts in the present, in order to verify the family's capacity to change with the help of the therapist's active intervention.

Psychodynamic therapists develop a particular ability to observe passively and to dole out their interventions cautiously. The interactional therapist's use of self is entirely different. He considers himself an active and reactive member of the therapeutic system, to which he contributes his personal creativity, inventiveness, and sense of humor, as well as his personal and professional experience. Physical contact and the utilization of space and movement are indispensable to the family therapist in observing functional and dysfunctional patterns of communication, personal and interpersonal boundaries, willingness to change, etc.

In interactional therapy, it is absolutely necessary to decipher the family's analogic language. An understanding of the group's nonverbal communications enables the therapist to *enter into* the system, that is, to learn the implicit rules of the group and to evaluate the degree of congruence between its verbal and nonverbal messages. The therapist, too, communicates analogically what his position is with respect to the group and to what extent he is willing to allow the family members to enter his personal space.

According to Duhl, Kantor, and Duhl (1973), the therapeutic system and space serve as a buffer for many families, and the therapist serves as an intermediary who facilitates communication and the transmission of new information. The objective of therapy is to produce learning that can be applied to other areas that remain outside the therapist's immediate control. For an interactional therapist, the spatial distribution of the family is highly significant. The way in which each member is seated supplies information concerning alliances, designations, centrality, and detachment. The "geographic" situation of the family is never casual, and it is the task of the therapeutic team to analyze it correctly.

In some cases, the way the family members situate themselves in space follows specific family rules. It may be considered a sort of X ray showing how relationships have been defined and codified in the group. The family may communicate this kind of information analogically from the very first moments of therapy. For example, we often find that the spatial situation of the identified patient differs from that of the others. Sometimes, in families who evade marital conflicts through overprotectiveness, the child designated as the identified patient occupies a very limited space between the parents, where he is clearly separated from the other siblings. In families who reject the "reprehensible" behavior of an adolescent, we are likely to notice that a considerable distance is established between this child and the rest of the family. The other members thereby express analogically their need to "keep their distance." In treating a couple, the spatial arrangement created by the partners supplies information on several levels: it indicates which partner requested therapy, which one feels he has been dragged into the situation against his will, which one has come only to accompany his "sick" partner, etc. Their positions in space probably also indicate the division of roles and functions between the partners. In general, by simply observing the space occupied by the members of a group, we can find out who is the group's leader, who is its official spokesman, who holds a peripheral position, etc.

It is important to remember, however, that the spatial positions taken by the family members, particularly in the phase in which the therapeutic system is being formed, are always influenced by the presence of the therapist, an outsider to whom the family has to adapt. Often, the spatial positioning of the family is determined more by the image that the group as a whole, or certain of its members, wish to present to the therapist than by their habitual patterns. In these cases, efforts by the family to demonstrate certain feelings or moods constitute a homeostatic reaction on the part of the system to the presence of an outsider who is felt to be threatening.

The therapist must enter into the family system in order to recognize fully the functional or dysfunctional interactional rules of its members. At this point, the context becomes effectively therapeutic. Although the spatial positioning of the family members is highly significant, this is true of the therapist's positioning as well. The therapist must situate himself in a privileged and neutral position with respect to the family. Any inexperienced therapist can easily lose his effectiveness and impartiality merely by situating himself inappropriately in space.

The utilization of space by the family members and the therapist can be an important criterion for evaluating therapeutic progress. Movement in the sessions is never casual; it is invariably indicative of interactive sequences. Therefore, the therapist elicits and observes movement, action, and play within the framework of this general therapeutic strategy, whose objective is to gather information, to dramatize and restructure unsatisfactory relationships, and to activate new patterns of interaction.

ACTION TECHNIQUES: SCULPTING

Family sculpting is one of the new nonverbal action techniques. It allows us to integrate systemic analyses with historical and inner aspects of the life of the individual and his family. In sculpture, inner psychic states and emotional relationships are symbolically recreated by representing the relationships between family members three-dimensionally, using bodies and movements.

We can define sculpture as the symbolic representation of a system, which utilizes the dimensions of space, time, and energy common to all systems. It permits participants simultaneously to represent and to experience relationships, feelings, and change.

However, it is as difficult to explain exactly what a family sculpture is as it is to describe a work of sculpture to someone who cannot directly observe the object itself.

Sculpting is a creative, dynamic, nonverbal modality in which the sculptor represents his own relationships to the members of his family group as well as the relationships existing among the other members at a given time and in a given context. The sculptor creates a spatial composition, which is often dramatic and which visually expresses his emotions and those of the members of his family as they interact.

We use the technique of family sculpting to gather information and for therapeutic purposes, as well as in training family therapists.

Methodology and Technique

The group activator (the therapist in a therapeutic system, or the trainer in a training group) invites the sculptor to place each member of the group in an appropriate position. The sculptor is asked to establish a particular distance or proximity between the actors and to assign them facial expressions and glances that symbolically reproduce his own personal perception of them and of their reciprocal relationships. He is also asked to place himself in the sculpture according to where and how he sees himself in relation to the others. The resulting composition condenses the most essential aspects of his past or present family experiences and projects them in a visible image.

It is usually the therapist who chooses the person who acts as sculptor. The other group members become the "clay," which the sculptor models and situates in space. In choosing the sculptor, the therapist takes into consideration both the particular phase of therapy and the characteristics of the family. For example, he may chose the person he thinks is most capable of spontaneously expressing his emotional experiences. Or, in other cases, he may choose the family member who seems most inhibited in communicating his feelings verbally. He may want to encourage this person to participate more actively by using nonverbal channels of communication. Or he may choose a child. Children may have greater facility and spontaneity in using action and movement to represent conflicts and family distress.

Once the sculptor has been chosen, the therapist helps him to begin. Often the novelty of the task creates emotional difficulties in the sculptor, who may feel blocked. Once the therapist has laid down the general rules and has gotten the process started, he becomes a participant-observer. He only occasionally comments on what is happening. While the sculpture is being created, words are used sparingly; in fact, words are used only to describe the position that each family member is asked to assume (and to describe the inner states that the sculptor wants to express through his choice of positions and postures). The participants are requested to take their parts in the representation without introducing glances, body positions, or movements of their own.

The efficacy of sculpting derives from the use of action rather than language to represent emotional situations. Sculpture goes beyond the expressive limits of words and liberates latent or unexpressed emotional states and communicational modalities. Sculpting family relationships enables us to size up the entire family situation "at a glance," both as a whole and in its individual parts. *Seeing relationships is the first step toward change*. This first "static" phase culminates in a "flash": when the sculptor has completed his sculpture, a sudden momentary pause occurs in which emotions and relations become "fixed" in space for the duration of a few seconds. The intensity of the representation is heightened, and the participants have an opportunity to grasp its essential characteristics. The participants talk about what they have experienced only after the sculpture has been terminated. It is interesting to note that at this point, verbal exchange among the participants becomes freer, more spontaneous, and more intimate.

In recent years, sculpting has been used more frequently as a therapeutic instrument. Movement in sculpting has been particularly emphasized. In fact, the term *sculpture* now seems inadequate to describe this modality. While this technique attempts to define the spatial and visual dimensions of relationships by means of a static, "sculptural" representation, it also translates emotional energies into movement (approach, separation). If the first step toward change is *to see the relationship*, the next step is *to move from one position to another*. Therefore, in the final dynamic phase of sculpting, the therapist may ask the sculptor or other participants how they feel in a particular position. Or he may en-

courage them to move to a more satisfying position or to adopt a different posture that they can maintain more comfortably. This stimulates the
participants to experiment with possible changes and allows the
therapist to verify how the family experiences these changes on an
analogic level. In fact, experimenting with movement and new positions
tends to open up new channels of communication and brings to light the
connections between the family structure (represented by the members'
spatial positioning), family interactions (represented by the members'
movements in relation to the structure), and emotional states (the feelings aroused by the various positions and movements attributed to the
individual members).

The nonverbal technique of family sculpting offers several advantages. Papp, Silverstein, and Carter (1973) emphasized, among other
advantages, that it avoids *rationalization, resistance, and stigmatization*.
Since members are deprived of their usual verbal channels, they are induced to communicate among themselves on a more significant level. In
fact, triangulations, alliances, and conflicts are represented in concrete
form and are situated in a visible, sensory, and symbolic sphere that
gives the participants an opportunity to communicate emotions to each
other at all levels.

Another advantage of sculpting is the *cohesive* effect it produces in
the family. The family members begin to think of themselves as a systemic unit, of which each member is an integral part that influences
every other part. I don't want to imply that it is necessarily better to
unite a family than to divide it. Keeping families together should never
constitute the preconceived goal of a family therapist. But I do want to
stress the importance of bringing family members to realize that it is they
who actively create their own system, and that the existence and the
rules of that system depend on the decisions of each member.

At the same time, representing oneself or being represented as part
of a system is a way of promoting greater individuation. Family sculpting is often an effective and unusual experience in enmeshed families,
where fusion and lack of identity and personal space form the matrix of
distress.

Family Sculpting

Once the principles of sculpting as a method of analysis and as a
form of nonverbal intervention are clear, it can be utilized in many ways
in both the diagnosis and the therapy of the family system.

The therapist can ask family members to sculpt the most important intrafamilial relationships or to represent the problem for which therapy has been requested. Or he can ask the identified patient to represent himself in his family role and the other members in relationship to this role. This leads the sculptor to act out openly certain stereotypes, and representing them in space often serves as an incentive to change. It also offers each member an opportunity to see himself as part of a system, integrated in a network of relationships and interactions, of which he normally is only partly aware. In particularly rigid family systems, representing dysfunctional relationships in space can have the same pragmatic effect as a paradoxical prescription. Behaviors that by definition are involuntary, spontaneous, and uncontrollable are made voluntary and can be repeated.

A family sculpture may reveal the family's ideal self-image by means of a "representation of desires": the sculptor is asked to model the family by structuring the relationships the way he would like them to be. When the results demonstrate a great disparity between the real sculpture and the ideal sculpture, the family is stimulated to work on its conflicts and to examine its expectations of itself and of therapy.

In working with a couple in conflict over the right to define the rules of their relationship, the therapist can invite the partners to sculpt the conflict. Immediately afterward, he can ask them to try out changes. For example, he can ask each partner in turn to define a personal space and a space for the other partner with respect to his own. He can then ask them, one at a time, to permit the partner to enter his or her space, experimenting with different modalities (for example, how this usually occurs, how they would like it to occur, how one partner thinks the other would like it to occur, etc.). Once these events have been acted out, the rules of the relationship become evident to both partners. The sculptor receives new information about how his behavior influences the other's behavior and vice versa. The physical and spatial representation of emotional states that were previously unrecognized or vague and confused can then be used to work out communicational modalities that are more congenial to both partners.

Sculpting is also very effective as a means of involving children in therapy. It offers them a "natural" medium for expressing emotions and significant relationships that could not be easily expressed verbally. It also gives children the feeling of how important their perceptions are to the adults (which makes them more willing to cooperate). Furthermore, sculpting often produces a dramatic visualization of the relationship between the symptom and family interaction.

Sculpting can also be used to represent the family's history by reenacting the life of the family from the past to the present. The therapist can ask the participants to sculpt their own nuclear families. He can then ask the parents to sculpt their families of origin. In this way, he can visualize the whole network of intrafamilial and extrafamilial relationships, as well as the relationships between present and past generations. This more complex vision of the larger network can help to promote greater differentiation of each person in his own reality context.

Parameters for Interpreting Sculpture

We analyze a family sculpture from a structural point of view in two separate phases: (1) in the *static* phase, in which the participants remain motionless in the positions assigned to them, crystallizing an image of familial relationships; and (2) in the *dynamic* phase, in which the participants move from one position to another, creating modifications in the group's usual patterns of relationships.

In the static phase, the positioning of the group members in space is important from a diagnostic point of view. Nicolò (1977) distinguished three types of sculpture:

1. Vertical (sculpture of attraction)
2. Horizontal (sculpture of escape)
3. Circular (sculpture of enmeshment)

A sculpture of attraction has a fixed center, which is represented either by a symbol or a person whom all members of the system recognize as having the power to define the relationship and/or to dominate the others. In patriarchal families, the center may be a member of undisputed authority, such as the father, the grandfather, or the memory of one of these. In other groups, it may be an ideology or a myth. Generally, the person who creates a sculpture of attraction tends to accentuate the vertical, spatial organization of the system. For example, he may position one member standing while he has all the others sitting at his feet. The lines of movement are usually centripetal.

A sculpture of escape is characterized by centrifugal lines of movement. The spatial distribution of the figures is horizontal, often moving laterally outward from one or more fixed centers. The fixed center may also be a space in the middle of the actors. This type of sculpture is common in families in which all members have a highly developed sense of autonomy (families that facilitate the emancipation of children).

However, a strong accentuation of the horizontal distribution and the centrifugal lines of movement can also be found in families who give inadequate attention to the needs of weaker members and who provide little security to any of the members. In these families, the individual and subsystem boundaries are particularly rigid and impermeable, and consequently there are difficulties in communication. Such families are like those Minuchin (1974) described as disengaged; the single members function autonomously, but they have an exaggerated sense of independence and lack feelings of belonging and ties to the system.

A sculpture of enmeshment calls to mind a particular type of pathological interaction. Each of the actors is conditioned by the behavior—or by the mere presence—of another person. Every relationship is a chain; the space is fixed and motionless; tension is high. The lines of movement are unclear and poorly expressed. At the moment of completion of the static phase, the spiral-like configuration of the group seems to create a barrier to the outside world. Within the sculpture itself, there is little distance between the individual members, and boundaries are confused. In the dynamic phase, the actors are incapable of clearly defining their lines of action. When they try to restructure the space, they eventually end up repeating the circular or spiral configuration present at the beginning. Sometimes one of the actors takes up a peripheral position, leaving the others to deal with the burden of the space left empty. This type of sculpture is most often seen in enmeshed families (according to Minuchin's terminology), in which the family system is so overloaded that it suffocates the resources needed for adaptation and change in circumstances of stress. The behavior of one member immediately arouses the affects of the others, and stress reverberates across the confused boundaries of every member.

From a dynamic point of view, according to the lines of movement in the sculpture and the utilization of space during a given unit of time, a sculpture can be (1) monochronic or (2) polychronic (Nicolò, 1977).

In general, we say that if everyone does the same thing at the same time and in the same way, the system is a monochronic block and the space is monochronic.

If in a given unit of time everyone does something different and in different ways, then the system is highly polychronic. If this tendency is carried to an extreme, the result may be dispersion, with the members escaping from the system. The system, in order to protect its very existence, reacts by reinforcing its own boundaries.

The monochronic or polychronic characteristics of the dynamic phase are interpretive categories that correspond to the family typologies we described in the discussion of the static phase.

Sculpture in Training for Family Therapists

Sculpture is also widely used in family therapy training programs. The future therapist sculpts the most significant relationships in his own family system, with the participation of the other members of the training group. He chooses the actors who represent the members of his real family from the group. Here, too, the static phase of the sculpture is followed by a dynamic phase of movement in which the sculptor and the actors search for new forms of expression and new ways of interacting. After the sculpture has been completed, considerable attention is given to the emotional reactions of the participants and to group discussion.

In training, *the sculpture of one's own family* can be carried out primarily for (1) the person who sculpts his family; (2) the actors who play the role of family members; or (3) the rest of the group (as observers).

As for the sculptor, representing the relationships in his own family promotes direct learning. The therapist frees himself from professional conceptualizations and stereotypes by shifting from the therapist-observer position to the position of director-actor of his own experiences. The more the therapist is able to expose himself to the group, to present himself in his family system, and to reveal his own difficulties in effectuating change, the more he will be able to understand the families he has in therapy. It will also be easier for him to convince families to represent their own interactional difficulties, which he will see as reversible, universal, and similar to his own.

In more general terms, family sculpting, besides permitting the therapist to explore his own family system, helps the members of the work group to get to know each other better and increases their intimacy. This is an important factor in a long training program that involves the participants emotionally and easily generates tensions and misunderstandings. Sculpting arouses attention and co-participation; each member feels that the others are interested in his story and in his problems.

Furthermore, the therapist who sculpts his own problems can decide either to have someone else impersonate him so that he can observe from the "outside," or he can experience the relationships that he wants to represent personally, from "within." This helps the future therapist bring to light and analyze dysfunctional interactional models that might otherwise be brought into his therapeutic practice without his being aware of it.

The sculptor's choice of group members to represent his family members is not casual. His choices reveal the type of relationship existing between the sculptor and the other group members. The sculptor's attribution of certain characteristics and roles to specific members of the group leads indirectly to change in the individuals and in their reciprocal relationships within the group. The observations made by the rest of the group after the sculpture is completed usually concern several aspects of the experience: (1) the family system that has been represented; (2) the sculptor involved in his creative activity; and (3) the individual group members who have taken part in the representation. But it is the presence of the group that supplies the structure and the temporal dimension of the action and gives a sense of history and continuity to the whole sequence. The group's presence also prevents the sculptor from entering into excessively intimate situations and, worse still, from presenting judgments concerning individuals.

Sculpting can also be used to represent other kinds of relationships beside familial ones. It is often used to promote growth in a group of therapists in training. In this case what is presented, by each member in turn, is the entire network of relationships existing in the group. The result is a sort of *group sculpture* that reveals interactional problems and the level of maturity and differentiation of each member in the group (which is seen as a system). It supplies a series of elements that help the members understand the history and evolution of the group. Sculpting is also useful for representing the therapist-supervisor relationship. This relationship between two people who are involved in the same task and who have complementary functions requires a dynamic process of growth. Sculpting can supply useful information about their relationship, about the degree of intimacy attained, and about their mutual expectations.

Sculpting also enables a therapeutic team to visualize the problems presented by a family in therapy and to evaluate the system's capacity for change. The team can impersonate the members of the family system and try out its particular transactional models in a sculptural representation. This experience can provide the team with information that is useful for evaluating factors such as the flexibility or rigidity of the system, possible alternative behaviors, and the degree of suffering experienced by the identified patient and other family members.

We often resort to this technique when we are working with families in crisis. Sculptural representations enacted by the therapeutic team make it possible to pinpoint the crisis in a spatial sequence, to visualize the various components in interactional terms, and to enter into the state of mind of the family members at the moment of crisis. This use of sculpture provides a more complete picture of the ongoing situation and suggests possible ways of intervening in the real situation.

Children and Play in Family Therapy

To understand the history and the present situation of a family system, we need to see the entire family group, including the children. Often a child is the best indicator of the affective situation of a family at a given moment. A child is able to express openly feelings and tensions that the parents are experiencing but are reluctant to reveal; he is often willing to support a sibling who is in difficulty; and he frequently indicates to the therapist the direction to take in therapy.

However, the presence of children in therapy poses a series of problems, and these may persuade an inexperienced therapist to exclude them from therapy. First of all, the presence of one or more children can easily create considerable confusion in the sessions. A therapist who does not easily tolerate children who move around or make noise will be prone to anxiety. He may feel that he is wasting time and failing to produce any "serious" results, or he may think that the parents disapprove of him for these reasons. Experience with large families has taught us that in a majority of cases, the motor activity and vivacity displayed by children offer the therapist an excellent opportunity for joining the family system, provided that he is able to utilize movement and action in interactional terms to create a common meeting ground between adults and children.

It is certainly not easy to interact appropriately with a family group. The disparity of age and interests among family members and the varying needs to which the therapist must respond require him to adapt continually to greatly differing behaviors and transactional patterns.

Often the therapist's fear of losing control over the situation leads him to exclude the children; he may justify his decision by reasoning that once marital problems are resolved, the symptomatic behavior of the children will automatically disappear. Sometimes a therapist is reluctant to include children in therapy because he wants to protect them or their parents. If he is eager to protect the children, he may want to exclude them early in therapy to avoid exposing them to certain topics or situations that may arouse their anxiety (this attitude merely reinforces family myths). If the therapist wants to protect the parents, he may make the same decision for fear that the children may precociously reveal dysfunctional areas within the family and cause negative reactions on the part of the parents. In either case, the therapist decides to work only with the couple, and he does not consider the children an integral part of the problem or its resolution.[1]

Another danger facing the therapist who includes children in therapy is that the therapeutic context may be too "adult." Children may be expected to understand concepts that are too abstract for them, or they may be asked to offer very logical responses or to remain seated for the entire session. This can occur if the therapist has not created an atmosphere in which the children feel free to express themselves in their usual manner and in which the adults feel free to communicate on a level accessible to the children.

On the one hand, the therapist must be able to stimulate confrontation between the adults and assure their cooperation in the therapeutic process; on the other hand, he must consider the child as *a person* who has every right to express and transmit thoughts, feelings, and opinions in his own idiom, without being treated as though he were subordinate or qualitatively inferior to the adults. The therapist, then, is required to *translate* different modes of thought: an adult mode, with its abstract concepts and predominantly verbal communication, and a child's mode, with its abundance of nonverbal expressions and concrete imagery.

Scientific interest in children's play was only aroused once it was acknowledged that children possess their own individuality and that they are not miniature adults. In the last 50 years, there has been much interest in child psychology, and many schools of psychoanalysis and

---

[1]"If family therapists lose the child's contribution as regulator of the speed of therapy, as moderator of the pace of change (through his "when and how" of symptom increase or decrease), the child fails to change" (Montalvo & Haley, 1973).

psychotherapy have developed psychodynamic theories of play. But very little experimental work has been done and not much has been written on play as a means of communication from a systemic perpective. Play is seen primarily as a means by which children express emotions and intrapsychic conflicts. Little attention has been given to the role of play as a transactional modality in child development or to the child-adult relationship in play. We are referring to the use of play not as an educational tool (as used by adults to transmit their expectations to children) but as a means by which adults and children learn to adapt to each other and to interact. In this sense, the role that the adult takes in play and the opportunities he offers to the child are of the utmost importance.

Play as a Means of Facilitating Children's Participation in Family Therapy

Play is the principal technique that makes it possible to include children in family therapy without treating them as miniature adults. Words constitute only one of the many ways in which a family system communicates. Even when children possess an extensive vocabulary, they continue to communicate through nonverbal modalities far more than adults do. Play represents a channel of communication of primary importance in working with children, although it can be used with adults as well.[2]

Play puts a child at ease; it makes the therapeutic context seem familiar to him; it allows him to express himself and to communicate his needs and moods to the others; and it also allows him to withdraw if the situation makes him feel anxious. Particularly at the beginning of therapy, the therapist should relate to the child through play. This makes the child feel that he is included in his own right, and he will be willing to cooperate. A therapy room that contains no toys, blackboard, drawing materials, or other objects familiar to the child seems cold and uninviting and makes him feel extraneous to what is happening. Of course, apart from toys and appropriate materials, the therapist has to know how to play; that is, he must know how to form a relationship

---

[2]In therapy with couples, we frequently use games as alternative means of communication, particularly in situations where verbalization invariably results in intellectualizing and rationalizing on the part of the couple, who use it to manipulate the therapeutic context.

through play. This is less obvious than it may seem. In reality, it is much easier to play in a dyadic therapist-child relationship than it is to engage a child in play in the presence of the whole family or to encourage adults and children to play together.

Encouraging children to play in therapy often induces adults to participate actively in the therapeutic effort. For example, if a father can be persuaded to take off his jacket and get down on the floor of the therapy room to play with his children, or if a nagging mother actually has fun in playing with her children, these parents will feel more optimistic and more motivated to work toward the goals of therapy, and the children too will collaborate more willingly.

Play as a Means of Joining a Family System

I have already stressed the importance of establishing contact with all family members and of making everyone feel at ease. This is not always easy, because the family may be very rigid or worried about some severe disturbance in a child or a parent. But even in these cases, play can provide access to the family group. Play can be used to redefine the therapeutic context and to change the affective tone of the whole family or some of its members.

I recall a home visit I made to an Italian-American family living in New Jersey. The paternal grandmother had also been invited. In earlier sessions, the parents had described this woman as a tyrant who continually interfered in their marital problems and in the education of their children. The request for therapy had been motivated by the rebellious and near-delinquent behavior of a 14-year-old son, who had obviously become the catalyst of family tension. In particular, he aroused the anger of the grandmother, who couldn't accept such behavior by a member of her family.

On this occasion, I played at length with Stefania, the 3-year-old daughter, as a means of joining the family system and befriending the grandmother. Stefania was the pet of the family, and everyone was very proud of her and affectionate to her. I took her on my lap and began to eat ice cream with her, playing "a spoonful for you, and a spoonful for me." I eventually managed to include the grandmother in the game, while the others observed with interest. By the time the game ended, the grandmother's initially sullen and suspicious attitude had visibly changed. She announced that she was ready to cooperate for the sake of the family. She began to offer useful information concerning the family's history and expressed her worries about the problem. This did not mean that the grandmother would not continue to interfere in the couple's marital life or in the children's education; nor did it mean that it would be easy to reestablish an equilibrium between the different generations in the family. Nonetheless the therapist had been implicitly accepted by the family, including its most authoritative member, and an emotional climate had been created that favored the beginning of the therapeutic process and improved the possibilities for success.

Another example that illustrates the use of play in an interactional framework concerns a family that had requested therapy because of the fears of a 13-year-old son. It was clear from the very beginning that the father, a worker at Fiat, strongly resented his son, whom he described as a complete "disaster," very insecure, and full of complexes. In this kind of context, questioning the boy about his father's statements would have increased his feelings of incompetence and made the system more rigid. First priority was given to redefining the context of the session. The therapist decided to do this by utilizing the energies of the father (until then he had contributed only unconstructive verbal interventions) and the son (who was participating through passive resistance) in a constructive way by playing a game. The therapist thought that this would promote an open and friendly confrontation between father and son and eliminate the accusatory and victimizing connotations of the situation. The therapist asked them to arm-wrestle. A physical confrontation would require active expression of their mutual hostility and direct physical contact, but it would also permit affective contact. The father could demonstrate his "competence" to his son, and the son could respond by accepting the challenge, thereby demonstrating self-confidence. The therapist, by acting as arbitrator, was able to enter more directly into the family system and was accepted by both father and son.

Play as a Means of Gathering Information about the Family System

If we look upon the family as a system of relationships, we must obviously gather information to identify the rules operating in the system at a particular moment. Reconstructing the history of a family group and analyzing its various elements in systemic terms is very different from putting together a case history out of cold and impersonal facts. Often verbal communication is not the richest source of significant information; clearly, it is emotionally more difficult to talk about delicate events and situations to a person who is felt to be a stranger rather than a friend.

The therapist must present himself in a friendly manner and should give particular importance to nonverbal communication, especially when speech serves more to hide facts and opinions than to reveal them. In this sense, play—like metaphor, the use of space, dramatization, and sculpture—helps the therapist to observe important family transactions in a context that is acceptable to the children and that does not make the parents feel that they are being judged.

Having a family play together or encouraging certain relationships through play is a way of gathering information. In the first place, the diligence with which the participants carry out an assigned task is an index of the credibility accorded the therapist. The family may intuitively perceive the play activity to be connected with the therapist's request for their active participation in the therapeutic process; or, on the contrary, they may feel that an invitation to engage in a play activity is ridiculous or out of place in the situation of distress that has brought them into therapy. Clearly, play that is activated in a therapeutic session is not an end in itself but contains the basic premises of a broader therapeutic strategy whose objective is to promote change.

Play also allows us to observe the rigidity of the family's designation of one of its members as "sick," as well as the relations between generations. If a family organizes an active game in which everyone takes part except the disturbed child, the designation is probably very rigid, and the family as a system (including the identified patient) probably feels threatened by any change—even temporary—in its way of defining itself. A rigid division among the siblings (which serves to prevent direct confrontation at the marital level) and consequent transgenerational alliances may be reflected in play by the repeated exclusion of some member or, more often, by a sharp division among the siblings. In these cases the child invariably chooses an adult rather than a sibling as his playmate. By observing the family engaged in a simple play activity, the therapist will receive data concerning the permeability of the system, the existence of dyadic ties between parents and children, and the degree of rigidity of the subsystems.

The Use of Play in Restructuring

The therapeutic function of play is discussed several times in this book, in terms of its metaphorical significance and as part of a prescription or of a broader strategy directed at provoking change in the rules of a family system.

I would now like to draw attention to the fact that play, with its great *simplicity* and *immediacy,* can be used in restructuring operations. If we transform the conflicts of a couple into a game, the visualization in a spatial dimension of an ambivalent or rigid pattern of interaction often leads to a dramatic realization by the participants of the existence of sentiments and behaviors that they have previously denied or of which they have been unaware. Furthermore, a game, by definition, requires the participants to respect a certain number of basic rules.

If the therapist has identified some of the system's dysfunctional rules and adopts them as the rules of a game, then the game is no longer a simple play activity. It exposes the limitations and the futility of certain ways of relating, and it encourages the participants to seek new transactional modalities and a more effective distribution of roles and family functions. This use of play is illustrated (in Chapter 4, p. 141) by the card game in which the rules dictated that the husband had to win and the wife had to allow him to win. This rule of the game forced the couple to exaggerate their usual interactive pattern.

Games can also bring to light the contradictory nature of messages in which literal and analogic levels of meaning are in contrast. In cases of this kind the therapist can propose a game in which only the explicit verbal message is utilized, while the implicit message, which usually disqualifies the former, is ignored. In the course of the game, the ambiguity of the message becomes embarrassingly evident; the previously hidden mystification is brought to light and clearly exposed to everyone. Once this has occurred, the participants have to seek a more constructive and less hypocritical way of interacting. Games also frequently reveal the crux of a problem without causing the participants to enter into a futile and exasperating escalation: since it is only a game, *there is no reason to take it so seriously.*

I will illustrate this concept with an example. The Lucarelli family requested therapy because their 10-year-old daughter, Daniela, had been caught stealing several times both at home and in a department store. The parents had different feelings and opinions about this problem. The father saw the facts as extremely serious and doubted that a remedy could easily be found. The mother tried to minimize the whole question and openly defended the daughter. The father seemed to play a central and authoritarian role in the family group. On the one hand, he lavishly praised his wife, describing her as an ideal companion and a capable mother; on the other hand, he totally boycotted her on an analogic level. His exaggerated opinion concerning the gravity of Daniela's problem seemed to be a pretext for implicitly accusing his wife of incompetence in educating the children, thereby strengthening his own claim to exclusive and incontestable authority. The wife seemed to lack self-confidence in her capacities as a mother (she talked at length about this during a session in which her husband was not present) and seemed unable to confront her husband openly in order to win greater autonomy for herself. Instead, she invariably supported him and accepted his praise, at least formally.

Both Daniela and her 11-year-old brother were vivacious and extroverted. They regularly showed initiative in inventing games to play together during the sessions. The therapist decided to intervene, utilizing a game that would confirm the literal level of the father's message (that his wife is competent) and also encourage the wife to express herself autonomously (leading to a contrast with the analogic level of her husband's message—which denied her competence). The therapist chose a game that would test the wife's actual competence. He asked the husband to observe from behind the one-way mirror and to take detailed notice of all of his wife's positive capabilities in playing with the children. The husband could surely not refuse this privileged role.[3]

The children were enthusiastic at the prospect of playing with their mother. The mother, with the therapist's encouragement, gained confidence in herself and had a good time participating in a creative game invented by the children. The mother and the therapist played the part of two customers dining together in a restaurant; the children were waiters who organized a song-and-dance show for the clients. The father, watching from behind the mirror, was nervous and not at all pleased by what was going on: the children were having a wonderful time with their mother, who in turn was feeling very much herself, amused, and seemingly uninterested in her husband's judgment. When the game was over and the husband was asked to give his opinion about his wife's capabilities, he remained silent, as though paralyzed.

[3]In clinical practice, we often divide the family in the sessions for tactical purposes. The one-way mirror can be used as a permeable diaphragm; it is an ideal means for encouraging certain kinds of interaction without provoking unwanted interruptions. Apart from its utility in exploring subsystems while blocking out potential intrusions by other family members, it offers to the latter an opportunity to *listen* to the needs of others and, implicitly, to search for more satisfactory ways of relating.

By accepting and emphasizing the literal level of the husband's message ("My wife is competent"), the game had made the analogic level of the message ("My wife is incompetent") seem untenable and absurd. In fact, the game confirmed the first message, which could not be negated because the second message, in order to exist, had to be explicitly negated. Thus the game made it impossible to maintain the contradiction that had prevented any change from occurring in the system and that had required the creation of a scapegoat to maintain a false harmony between parents. Furthermore, the game had given the mother an opportunity to experience her own competence in dealing with her children and to feel accepted by them. This gave her the courage to reject her subordinate and submissive role. In the past, her behavior had reinforced her husband's need to control the family and had helped to perpetuate a vicious circle.

4

Tasks

Directiveness in Family Therapy

The practice of giving instructions to patients is a form of behavior at least as ancient as the concept of healing itself. Although it is often difficult to recognize—and to accept—that therapeutic relationships are directive, there is no doubt that all types of therapy are fundamentally directive.

When we prescribe drugs to a person suffering from anxiety, when we remain silent until a patient begins to produce free associations, when we advise sending an inhibited child to summer camp, when we teach a couple how to achieve orgasm, when we prescribe paradoxical behavior, or even when we refuse to provide therapy because we feel that the basic elements of a problem are not of a psychological nature—in each case our behavior is directive.

Psychoanalysis, Rogerian therapy, and psychodynamic therapies have led us to believe that the patient must decide what is to happen in the session. But, in fact, the therapeutic context, the implicit rules of the relationship, the use of space, the capabilities of the therapist, and his interventions are all signs of a relationship in which the therapist holds a position of power and directiveness that is officially accepted by the patient.

Family therapy, like every other strategic therapy, is undeniably directive. However, the kind of directiveness involved is different from that common to psychodynamic therapies. In family therapy, the therapist, together with the family, is actively engaged in creating an evolving context, setting goals, planning interventions, evaluating the group's responses to his directives and modifying these if necessary, and working toward the disengagement of the family at the termination of the therapeutic process.

Some critics consider these aspects of family therapy *manipulative*: they think that the family may lose its capacity for self-determination or that it may be forced to assume inappropriate responsibilities. If family therapy actually produced these effects, their criticism would be justified. Indeed, interactional therapy (or any other kind of therapy) can produce undesirable results of this kind if undertaken by therapists who lack a profound respect for the freedom of the individual and the acute sensitivity necessary to an understanding of the problems of a family in its social context.

Family therapy attempts to develop the capacities of family groups for self-determination. Families are frequently immobilized in difficult situations that they seem unable to overcome except through the creation and maintenance of scapegoats. If the family continues to use its habitual models of thought and behavior, it will find it impossible to change. Knowing this, the family therapist believes that his initial task is *to make breaches* in the family system. He upsets the *status quo* to enable the family group to rediscover its own self-therapeutic capacities, to liberate the identified patient and the entire family from long-standing suffering, and to restore initiative to the family itself. An operation of this kind requires the therapist to work from a position of *power*, for he must immediately confront the most rigid forces operating in the system. Often this confrontation leads to what Carl Whitaker has described as the "battle for control." From the very beginning of therapy, the therapist must demonstrate to the family that he is strong enough to control the family successfully. He must be able to maintain a one-up position consistently.

This battle for control permits the family group to judge whether the therapist is strong enough to support it during an eventual process of change. If the therapist is not capable of leading—that is, of dictating the rules of the relationship consistently—he will eventually be sucked into the habitual transactional models of the family; the family will not accept him as an effective agent of change and will probably interrupt the therapy.

Although the therapist must assume a position of control in the initial phase of therapy, the therapeutic relationship should be completely transformed at the conclusion of therapy. Then, family and therapist hold equal power, because the family group has regained its full capacity to determine its own actions and no longer requires outside help.

At this point, it is important to specify in what way interactional therapy is directive and what its goals are. The mere act of bringing together an entire family, of involving a family nucleus in an operation requiring direct confrontation and a process of reciprocal learning, is in itself directive. Asking for the active commitment of the members of a group in seeking a solution to a problem within or outside of the family system and rejecting attempts to delegate the responsibility to the "expert" are also directive maneuvers.

It is easy, too, to see how the therapist, by the way he uses space and movement and assigns tasks in the sessions, communicates that he is the person who is guiding the therapeutic process. Moreover, his directive function in therapy is further emphasized by his consultations with the supervisor during the sessions.

It is also important to define what we mean by *change*,—the goal of every therapy—in a systemic approach. Change means more than the resolution of the symptoms of an individual: it means deeply affecting all members of the system by offering them new transactional models that eliminate the need for symptomatic behavior. Symptoms are seen as signals of a disturbance in communication. An intervention that focuses on a symptom automatically implies changing the system's rules of communication.

The views of Papp, Silverstein, and Carter (1973) on how actions are translated into insight are similar to Erikson's. They maintain that insights that do not produce behavioral change in the family system are meaningless. According to these therapists, changes in family relationships may in some cases occur as a result of changes in emotional relationships or through new insights; but in other cases, they may not occur at all.[1]

In many kinds of therapy, we frequently make the mistake of assuming that if someone *understands* something, he will behave in a way that is consistent with this understanding. In the practice of therapy, we more frequently find that if a person *changes* in some respect, he will be

[1]A family in therapy may be incapable of undertaking a new course because it seems too risky or too demanding in terms of commitment. Nevertheless, the fact that the family has learned through concrete experience that alternative solutions previously unrecognized or denied do exist is in itself of considerable therapeutic value.

able to experiment and thereby to learn alternative modes of cognition, feeling, and behavior. According to Wittgenstein (1956), *restructuring*[2] does not call attention to something (that is, it does not produce insight); it teaches a new game, thereby making the old one lose its appeal. Although I think it is true that we can often produce change by trying out new modes of problem solving in a given situation, I do not exclude the possibility that such change may be related to insight. There seems to me to be no simple answer to the question of whether change is produced by insight or whether insight is achieved contemporaneously or as a consequence of change.

Classification of Tasks

A task can be formulated on the basis of work done in the sessions, of interactional information that has been gathered, or of material brought in by members of the family system. Tasks can be assigned to involve, directly or indirectly, the whole family or only some of its members. Some tasks are to be carried out in the sessions, others in the intervals between sessions.

Giving directives in therapy is a form of strategic intervention that serves several purposes. In general, the assignment of a task is used *to promote change*, that is, to activate new transactional patterns that do not require the creation or maintenance of scapegoats. In particular, tasks help to *create a therapeutic context* by establishing a collaborative atmosphere in which certain general rules are respected, thus avoiding victimizing, tyrannical, or accusatory behavior, the delegation of responsibility to the therapist, and the maintenance of stereotyped roles. By behaving directively, the therapist interacts intensely with the family. By functioning as guarantor of each member's autonomy and subjectivity, he acquires importance in the eyes of the family. He will be able *to join the family system* and to gain acceptance by all of its members by refusing to become involved in implicit or explicit alliances or coalitions with any of the members. Tasks given as "homework" are intended *to amplify the therapeutic process* beyond the hour of the weekly meeting with the family and to make the therapist's "presence" in the family felt in the sphere of daily life. In this way, the family can *try out new ways of communicating*: if it succeeds in using these "for the sake of therapy," it

[2]Briefly, this term refers to the elaboration of different interactional patterns, utilizing preexisting elements.

will gradually feel more capable of functioning autonomously and will eventually no longer need therapeutic support.

In working with particularly rigid systems (families with a schizophrenic or anorectic member), I have found that by assigning tasks I can lengthen the interval between sessions to two weeks, a month, or even three months. Therapy conducted in this way can still be effective once the therapist has joined the family system, successfully discovered its dysfunctional rules, and then prescribed these same rules to the family (see p. 127). The success of this paradoxical technique depends more on the therapist's skill in uncovering the rules that the family tries so hard to conceal than on the task itself. Sometimes this can be extremely difficult. But if the therapist succeeds, he wins the family's confidence. And once the cards are out on the table, the family is finally able to play a new game. Creating a new set of rules for itself makes the family feel responsible for its own transformation.

Furthermore, the way in which a task is carried out *provides interactional information* concerning the family's structure and the reactions of its members to requests for change. In many cases, the correct performance of the task itself is less important than the analysis of the reactions of the family members involved. A task must be performed, not interpreted: the family group must be induced *to experience an operative interactional situation*. This reduces the probability that the family will utilize verbal and rational defenses that might prolong therapy. That is, tasks prevent the family from building up defenses before even trying something "different."

We are not implying that by making action precede verbalization we can avoid the emergence of resistances; on the contrary, resistances are likely to emerge more rapidly and explicitly.

In addition, the assignment of a task always has *significance as communication for the family members*. They speculate on what message is concealed behind the therapist's requests and formulate hypotheses concerning themselves or the others. The therapist must keep this in mind in formulating a task and in analyzing how it is carried out.

The following outline, which categorizes the various kinds of tasks, is based on my work with families. It has been worked out together with my collaborators.[3]

[3] I am particularly grateful to Paolo Menghi, with whom I discussed and elaborated on a great deal of this material. Many of the examples described in this chapter are drawn from clinical work done together with Menghi, Nicolò, and Saccu.

I. Restructuring Tasks
  A. *Countersystemic* tasks (used to oppose the homeostasis of the family system directly).
  B. *Contextual* tasks (used to establish or maintain a therapeutic context).
  C. *Displacing* tasks (used to displace the problem artificially from the identified patient to another family member or to a new symptomatology).
  D. *System-restructuring* tasks (used to restructure existing interactional patterns, utilizing elements in the system).
  E. *Reinforcing* tasks (used to reinforce tendencies that are already active in the family system and that are capable of promoting change).
  F. Tasks utilizing the symptom (tasks of *attack* or *alliance*).
II. Paradoxical Tasks
  A. *Prescribing the symptom* (used to prescribe disturbed behavior).
  B. *Prescribing the rules* (used to solicit the participation of the entire family by prescribing the system's idiosyncratic rules).
III. Metaphorical Tasks

Restructuring Tasks

The term *restructuring* is used to denote a process in which the habitual transactional patterns of the family are modified by using elements and energies present (at least potentially) in the system. The system thereby takes on new characteristics; it changes, although the elements of which it is composed remain the same.

This concept, which is of central importance in our approach, is also applicable to paradoxical tasks. The distinction lies in the fact that in paradoxical tasks, restructuring occurs indirectly as a consequence of changes brought about by the use of a therapeutic paradox, whereas restructuring provokes immediate changes.

The question of what to consider in order to choose which type of directives to use cannot be answered unless we first analyze restructuring and paradoxical tasks in detail.

Countersystemic Tasks

Often this modality of intervention reflects the therapist's lack of experience rather than an appropriate choice of strategy. The inexperienced therapist, who bases his judgment on *contents* rather than on the underlying *interactional patterns*, may try to oppose the homeostasis of the family system overtly. As a result, he finds himself struggling with inadequate means against the family's tendency to preserve the *status quo*.

This category of tasks includes all of those kinds of therapeutic advice based on an oversimplified view of a situation. Such advice aims at soliciting change in the identified patient, who is asked to rely on the very energies that he feels he does not possess, or at preventing the family members from persisting in behavior that the therapist considers unconstructive or detrimental. In this kind of approach the therapist finds himself opposing—or ignoring—the systemic dynamics of the group in question.

An approach of this kind may ultimately result in the creation of a context of accusation or futile competition. This produces a negative effect on the identified patient and on the other family members, and it eventually undermines the family's confidence in therapy.

Contextual Tasks

Contextual tasks are carried out during the sessions and are used *to promote the formation and maintenance of a therapeutic context*.

The objective of such tasks is to provide concrete, operative experiences during the sessions; they are often utilized to obtain a *change* in an atmosphere that the therapist feels is inappropriate to that particular phase of therapy. For example, contextual tasks are assigned to modify an accusatory or hyperprotective situation existing at the beginning of a therapy. Here, the task is used to promote respect for the autonomy of each individual and to make clear that each member is responsible and important in the family.

In fact, it often happens that the identified patient is deprived (or deprives himself) of self-affirmation and individual freedom. A child or an adolescent may not even be consulted about undertaking therapy. He may not even be asked to reply to questions that directly concern him or to express his own desires.

The therapist can request silence when one family member tries to interrupt another, or he can actively engage a member who remains in a marginal position in the therapeutic process by offering him "space" and adequate support. He can divide the family into subgroups if he thinks this will give some member greater opportunity to express himself more freely, or he can ask an overly intrusive member to observe from behind the one-way mirror.

He can also solicit particular interactions by directing two or more persons to discuss or to do something together during the session. This may provide a new experience for the family and elicit cooperation, thus preparing the way for successive interventions.

Not infrequently in the course of therapy, once positive change has been produced the family may counteract by attempting to return to a preceding homeostatic level. In such cases, contextual tasks can help to stabilize change, even in advanced phases of therapy.

Displacing Tasks

If we assume that a scapegoat role is functional to a particular system at a particular moment, then we can hypothesize that the presence of a second patient or a new symptomatology will create significant movement within the system. Displacing tasks are intended *to displace the problem artificially from the scapegoat to another family member*. In fact, evidence indicates that once the identified patient has been removed from his central position and the symptomatic area has been desensitized, it is easier to trigger a process of change by encouraging the utilization of healthier transactional modalities.

A displacing task brings about a transition from an abnormal situation for which the family has requested an intervention to another situation of abnormality that is new and artificial. This second, temporary situation is created by the therapist to promote change by disrupting the homeostatic balance of the family system and increasing the number of variables and possible alternatives. The evaluation of a problem differs when another problem, which may be more acute or more pressing, emerges. The new factor brings about a new alignment of forces and requires the persons involved to reevaluate the significance of the original problem. A redistribution of family functions is automatically called for, and this makes it easier to adopt new models of interaction. In order to create a displacement, the therapist can amplify some minor disturbance mentioned by a family member, or else he can create a problem *de novo*. The new problem, since it is artificial, is needed for a limited time only and can be easily resolved once change has been introduced. The task can be assigned and carried out either in *alliance* with the chosen "second patient" or without his knowledge.

Let's consider the case of Luciano (see Chapter 5). Luciano is 16 years old and an only child. He has suffered from phobias for years. His tyrannical and aggressive behavior in the family corresponds to his fear of facing the world outside of the home. He has always slept in his parents' bed. For the last three years the father has been sleeping in the living room while Luciano, who is afraid of sleeping alone, sleeps with his mother. He left school in the seventh grade, and he has never worked, although he has frequently stated that he is ready to look for a job.

Five months have elapsed since the start of therapy, and the question of Luciano's autonomy has become particularly urgent. After a session dealing with the problem of sleeping arrangements, the therapists realize that a redefinition of generational boundaries in this situation (restoring Luciano to his role as son and working simultaneously with the couple) is a premature objective. Luciano verbalizes what the therapists have supposed: "The problem of sleeping will be the last step in getting well. I'll get over everything else first; that will be the last step."

At this point in the therapy, we decide to deal with Luciano's autonomy outside of the family by using a strategy that momentarily transfers the *disturbances* from Luciano to his father. We decide to assign a task related to the father's only sphere of outside activity: his job. The father has been a salesman in a department store for 20 years, and he has never missed a day's work. His work constitutes perhaps the only area of his life that gives him real satisfaction and in which his competence is generally appreciated by everyone, including his wife and son.

One of the two co-therapists speaks to the father separately and requests his collaboration in stimulating Luciano to undertake some form of responsibility outside of the home. The task consists in taking a two-week leave of absence from his job. He is directed to stay at home, to behave in an unusually depressed and negligent manner, and to refuse contact with the rest of the family. The therapists warn him that it will not be difficult to behave as though he is depressed: in two weeks at home, he will learn much about important and upsetting aspects of family roles and functions. The father agrees to cooperate.

This therapeutic move cannot fail to evoke a strong reaction, particularly in Luciano. In the following session, Luciano attacks the therapists, whom he holds responsible for his father's illness. He also communicates his decision to become the alternative valid member of the family: "If he is in this state, then it's up to me to take the family in hand!"

The task has temporarily disrupted the equilibrium of the family system and has activated new processes. Luciano, after personally contacting several people, begins to work. He no longer comes to the sessions, although he sends reassuring messages to the therapists via his parents, and he gradually begins to participate in the recreational activities of a group. At the same time, the spouses, without Luciano, begin to confront each other over long-neglected marital problems. Our directives in this case were certainly unusual, but effective: they served to initiate a process of emancipation in Luciano and of confrontation between his parents.

The displacement of the symptom is not always artificial. In some cases it calls attention to another real problem. This change in focus may destabilize the system by increasing the number of variables and by compelling the family to redefine the presenting problem.

The case of Adriano illustrates this kind of displacement. Adriano, the identified patient, was 28 years old and the youngest child in a large family. Relations between family members were highly protective and intrusive.

The death of the father 20 years earlier had created confusion in the generational boundaries. The eldest son, Romano, age 45, had assumed parental functions. In some ways, he had also become a partner to his mother. The mother regarded him with particular respect, and she frequently called him by his father's name. Romano claimed that his paternal functions had prevented him from thinking enough about himself. In particular, he had been unable to make a decision concerning his relationship with a female friend. This relationship, which he maintained for many years, seemed in some ways typically adolescent. Romano saw his girl friend frequently, but always at her house, even though he had an apartment of his own (he used his apartment only for storage and he actually lived with his family). He slept with her only occasionally. When this happened, he would bring along clothing which he then took home to be laundered.

The other children were Mario, age 40, Loredana, age 38; Isabella, age 35; and Adriano. The last three were employed but living at home. They all agreed that they were a very close family and that they had few outside interests. Mario, the second eldest, had created an independent existence with a family of his own and lived away from the home. During the course of the therapy, both the mother and the other children repeatedly described Mario as insensitive and "different" from the rest of the family.

Family therapy was requested after a suicide attempt by Adriano, which the rest of the family saw as completely incomprehensible. Adriano had tried to hang himself and had been saved at the last moment by Romano. Adriano had no psychiatric precedents. The family described him as the youngest and most sensitive member of the family. For this reason the family had always been particularly attentive to him.

Following this very serious incident, the family system was more "united" than before and became even more protective and stifling. The family began to observe Adriano's every move, even the most innocent. Whereas previously each family member had lived "for" the others, after this incident the whole family began to live exclusively "for" Adriano. For his part, Adriano seemed incapable of reacting to this stifling control; in fact, he tried to justify it, interpreting it as the highest proof of the family's love for him (the others, of course, agreed with this interpretation).

After a few exploratory sessions, the therapist realizes that keeping attention focused on Adriano and his problems produces the kind of situation that occurs when a football team gathers around the ball: the space is closed and there is no way to get out. Therefore, the therapist decides to break up the protective circuit by *displacing the problem* to Romano, who is clearly highly ambivalent about his continued presence in the family home.

At this point, the therapist draws everyone's attention to Romano. He starts calling him by his father's name and he "convinces" him that his young (!) brother and sisters and his mother are completely dependent on him in this dramatic period. The therapist stresses the point by confirming the inability of Adriano and his sisters to take care of themselves (the younger siblings have in some ways remained "fixated" at an adolescent level of development, corresponding to their ages at the time of their father's death. This fixation allows Romano to continue his paternal role).

Utilizing the information gathered during the first sessions, the therapist confirms and exaggerates Romano's competence and the incompetence of the others to such an extreme that the therapist makes them seem ridiculous. The tactic of shifting attention from Adriano to Romano has a specific goal: it gives the therapist greater control over potential homeostatic reactions by the systems, and at the same time it allows him to attack the system's dysfunctional rules. The system feels threatened because its game has been revealed and prescribed, and it reacts accordingly. The family members seek greater cohesion among themselves in order to convince the therapist that their roles are not really so rigid now that they are all adults.

As the system begins to lose its stability, the therapist reinforces his strategy in order to accelerate the process. He insistently encourages Romano in his role as father substitute, and he belittles the efforts of Adriano and the two sisters to achieve independence. He maintains that these efforts are immature and that they only confirm the need for Romano to cut off his relationship with his girl friend and to remain home and devote himself exclusively to the family. The mother agrees with the therapist's instructions and is eager to collaborate, as she hopes to regain Romano as a partner. In this way, a temporary displacement has been achieved: the new problem is Romano, and everyone must help him return to his role as the principal support of the family. This intervention is obviously paradoxical and it implicitly challenges the system: the younger siblings have to help Romano (thereby behaving as adults) so that Romano can continue to act as the leader of the family (although this is no longer really necessary).

This strategy puts Romano in difficulty: he is afraid that he may never be able to leave the family and build a life for himself. This fear increases and becomes more concrete in therapy, thereby making his desire for autonomy more acute. By moving attention away from Adriano's suicide attempt and onto the family's need for Romano as a "father," the therapist has only apparently modified the therapeutic goal. In reality, Adriano's suicidal behavior had served as a signal of the real problem: the children's need for autonomy and the family system's inability to tolerate the separation of its members. By displacing the symptom, the therapist is able to prescribe the rules of the system, justifying this operation as a response to Romano's needs.

The task is articulated in two successive and complementary phases: the first part of the task is paradoxical and is intended to exacerbate the existing system of control and the generational confusion. Romano is instructed to take the family in hand and to give up all external distractions. He is asked to make his mother report to him daily about Adriano's behavior. He is to telephone home from work several times a day to make sure that all is well. He is also told to prevent his sisters from fighting because this might have deleterious effects on Adriano. Romano is instructed to keep detailed written records of all of these things and to bring his notes to be analyzed in the sessions.

The system reacts promptly: Romano becomes more dissatisfied with a role that restricts his autonomy. Adriano and the sisters feel that they are being treated like children, and they begin to say that the family can manage perfectly well without Romano. They insist that Romano should lead his own life. The mother is the least resentful, but she unexpectedly begins to express concern that Romano may not get married, and then "who will take care of him after I'm dead?"

The therapist assigns the second part of the task when he thinks the system has been sufficiently destabilized and that it will not be able to return to the previous *status quo*. At that point, he instructs Romano to leave home for a month and to go to live with his girl friend. He is told that he will be allowed to telephone his mother once a day to find out *only from her* how the situation is. He is also told not to bring his clothes home to be laundered or to go home for any other reason whatever. The therapist tells him that a month away from home will make him realize how *indispensable* he is to the family. After this experience, he will have no further doubts as to where his future lies; his mother will surely have him back again.

The therapist predicts that Adriano's situation may worsen and that he may make another suicide attempt. He also predicts that the sisters will become more nervous. Romano, however, is asked not to intervene in any way. The therapist reassures the family, and particularly the mother, that a team from the center will be available day and night in case of emergency. The mother is instructed to take over Romano's task of noting down Adriano's behavior as well as the fights between the sisters during Romano's absence.

The second phase of the task is intended to consolidate the patterns introduced in the earlier phase. It promotes a different relationship between the single members of the family and between Romano and the family, and at the same time it denies that Romano's exit from the scene represents an alternative basis for a new systemic equilibrium. By predicting that Adriano will get worse, the therapist blocks the possibility of a relapse.

If Romano proves capable of maintaining greater distance, and if the family can accept this without demanding his protection, then the system will be able to experience the advantages of different ways of relat-

ing and allow all of the members greater autonomy—despite the fact
that Adriano's suicide attempt seemed to have reduced opportunities for
self-determination at this time.

System-Restructuring Tasks

The goal of these tasks is to *restructure* the models of communication
habitually used by the family. Restructuring is achieved by substituting
new and more functional communicational patterns arrived at through
an exploration of elements and energies existing in the system.

The case of Sandro (see page 34) contains several examples of tasks
whose objective is to provoke systemic restructuring. When the
therapist requests that during the session father and son negotiate issues
concerning the boy's emancipation, the task becomes a concrete method
of restructuring the patterns of coalitions and divisions in the system.
Any agreement intended to reevaluate Sandro's maturity must be
worked out in the light of the functional aspects of his immaturity.

By examining the effects of this agreement, session by session, the
process of exploration begun in the therapeutic sessions is made operative at home. Father and son become engaged in daily efforts to honor
an agreement that has been officially sanctioned by all. The mother and
the aunt have to cooperate in the actuation of a plan that involves them
as well. They are particularly eager to demonstrate that their behavior
toward Sandro is correct and not protective, as the father has stated.

Once a process of systemic reorganization has been initiated, it is
easier to broaden the field of intervention to include difficulties and
needs that are less directly connected with the problem for which
therapy was requested. This stage marks a turning point in the process
of growth and differentiation within the family group.

Another, much simplified example of *systemic restructuring* shows
how this strategy can promote a rapid reappraisal of the presenting
problem.

Mrs. Maggi comes to therapy together with her 5-year-old daughter
and a baby-sitter. The baby-sitter remains in the waiting room. Mrs.
Maggi has been separated from her husband for two years and is living
with her child and the baby-sitter. The presenting problem concerns the
daughter, Silvia, whom the mother describes as uncontrollable and immature for her age. The underlying problem comes to the surface
quickly: it concerns the mother's ambivalent relationship with her hus-

band (from whom she has not been able to separate emotionally) and her present situation as a woman alone. She speaks in a theatrical manner and continually confuses the problems of her child with her own existential dilemma. The child's areas of autonomy are continually invaded by the mother, who has managed to involve Silvia totally in her own conflicts. Silvia's behavior is indeed despotic and erratic, but despite her mother's complaints, there is evidently some form of complicity between them. Maria, the baby-sitter, should leave the mother considerable freedom by relieving her of at least part of her child-care duties. But in fact she has no power at all over the child (the child refuses even to play with her), which creates a further problem. The mother's relationship with the baby-sitter is similar to that with her daughter: she oscillates between comradeship and intrusiveness and worries about whether she is adequately fulfilling her responsibilities toward the baby-sitter, who is still young.

The first session, while not very productive in dealing with the problems presented by the mother, is very important for the therapist: it clarified the problems so that they can be dealt with in future sessions. The therapist asks Silvia and Maria to go into another room where they are to prepare a song and dance to perform for the mother. In the meantime, the therapist engages the mother in a discussion of problems that do not concern the others. After the agreed time has elapsed, Maria and Silvia return to the therapy room and present their "number," while the mother, sitting to one side with the therapist, observes with interest and amusement.

With a very simple task, the therapist has traced a boundary between mother and child, thus restructuring their respective areas according to their different needs.

Silvia's symptomatic behavior has been reduced by activating the relationship between the child and the baby-sitter in creative play. This interactive pattern enacted in therapy can be repeated at home. The mother's problem, which had been misunderstood and confused with her daughter's behavioral problems, finally appears in its own right. This permits us to begin to redefine the goals of therapy.

Reinforcing Tasks

Reinforcing tasks are those used to strengthen movements that are already under way in the family system and that are thought to be useful in obtaining change.

It is clear that contextual, displacing, and system-restructuring tasks can also act as reinforcers insofar as they tend to promote solutions that have begun to take form within the family group.

In these cases, the therapist need only encourage processes that the family has set in motion by virtue of its own self-therapeutic potential. There may be moments when the tendencies toward change temporarily outweigh the homeostatic tendencies. Here, the therapist need only formulate a directive that acknowledges, enlarges, and articulates what is already taking place. If the family members perceive that their own movements are in harmony with the therapist's instructions, they will increase their efforts to collaborate, thus increasing the probability of achieving the goals of therapy and shortening its duration.

Reinforcing tasks serve to consolidate changes that have already taken place and to promote further change. They are frequently utilized during the last phase of therapy. The family is assigned a task to be performed at home and is asked to come to the following session, not to discuss their problems, but to demonstrate to the therapist (and to themselves) that the work done in therapy has been effective over a period of time.

A reinforcing task is used in the case of the De Angeli family (described in Chapter 2, p. 63) after four months of weekly sessions.

After evaluating the results already obtained, the therapist asks the family to come back three months later. He tells the family to use this period to consolidate their progress and to work on other problems mentioned by the family. The therapist adds, however, that the following meeting can take place only if each member feels that the others have collaborated in carrying out the task. Otherwise the session will be postponed one more month.

The task is in itself a positive reinforcement: the family has to return to the therapist only to inform him that they no longer need him. In this way, the family will feel responsible for its own transformation.

About a month before the date set for the next session, the father telephones the therapist to report that there are problems between the mother and Laura, and he asks to have another session earlier than planned. The therapist is firm. He points out that it is against the rules to telephone and reminds the father of the terms laid down for holding the next session.

The following sequences are from the session held at the end of January, as originally planned. The entire family participates.

THERAPIST (*smiling*): The last time we met was. . . .

FATHER: We met. . . .

MOTHER: In November. . . .

LAURA: Yes, the first week of November.

THERAPIST: Then three months have gone by. Have you followed the rule about coming back only if each of you is satisfied with the progress that's been made?

FATHER: Yes. After all, we are serious people.

THERAPIST: Can you demonstrate your seriousness?

FATHER (*seeking guidance*): What task are you going to give us?

THERAPIST (*smiling*): I want you to conduct the session this time. I am just going to watch and observe what improvements you have made.

FATHER: We have made improvements. . . .

LAURA: Can I write them on the blackboard?

THERAPIST: Why not? Just the way we did before. It helps us remember them better.

FATHER: First of all, write down our relationships. The relations between Mom and Dad. (*to his wife*) We are getting along much better. There's more discussion between us. When a problem comes up, we talk about it, we argue about it, and we solve it. I think my wife and I are more mature than we were. Anyway, we are on the right road.

THERAPIST (*good-humoredly*): I bet you were the kind of student who got top grades on exams!

FATHER: Me? No . . . and relations with our daughters are. . . .

THERAPIST (*to the father*): Wait a minute, please don't go so fast. We were talking about you and your wife. (*to the mother*) Mrs. De Angeli, what do you think about this?

MOTHER: Oh, I agree with my husband, especially now that we have more dialogue.

THERAPIST: You mean that you talk. . . .

MOTHER: Yes.

THERAPIST: Before, you talked less. . . .

MOTHER: Much less. We didn't talk about little things or about important things. Now, maybe we don't agree on some things, but we find a way of getting along anyway.

THERAPIST (*expressing incredulity*): You have managed to do this in just three months?

MOTHER: We had already begun earlier. . . .

THERAPIST: That's true. You mean that you have consolidated the improvements.

MOTHER: Yes, exactly.

FATHER: Particularly in these last months, with everyone contributing.

THERAPIST: Do you mean including the grandmothers?

FATHER: No, I'm really referring to our family. We don't talk much about the grandmothers anymore.

MOTHER: But some relations have been broken off pretty abruptly. That bothers me somewhat.

THERAPIST: For example?

MOTHER: For example, with my mother.

THERAPIST: Don't you ever see her?

MOTHER: Rarely.

THERAPIST: When was the last time you saw her?

MOTHER: At Christmas.

FATHER: Yes, we were with her on Christmas Day. Now we do other things on Sundays. I take the older girls to a soccer game, or else we all go to the mountains.

THERAPIST (*to Laura and Marina*): Do you like watching soccer games?

LAURA and MARINA (*together*): Oh, yes, we love it!

THERAPIST: Before, you didn't go to soccer games or to the mountains! Isn't that true?

FATHER: I went to watch soccer by myself.

MOTHER: And I stayed home and faced . . .

THERAPIST (*to the mother*): Now that you stay home with just Claudia, you have more peace and less work to do.

MOTHER: That's right.

THERAPIST: And when you go to the mountains, who goes? Just the family?

LAURA: No, we go with other people.

FATHER: We go with friends.

THERAPIST: You didn't do that before.

LAURA: We used to go alone, just the family used to go, and it was less fun.

THERAPIST: Oh! So now you go with other families, with other kids your age!

LAURA: Yes.

THERAPIST: I think you once told me that all your friends were younger than you. Do I remember correctly?

LAURA: Yes. That's right.

THERAPIST: But now you have friends your own age. . . .

LAURA: Yes, I have girl friends and boy friends, both.

THERAPIST: They're mixed.

LAURA (*laughing*): Yes.

MOTHER: And even the invitations are . . .

THERAPIST: Mixed! (*Everyone laughs.*)

MOTHER: She gets invitations . . . I don't know . . . like to go out for pizza on Saturday night.

THERAPIST: I'm afraid the blackboard isn't big enough. Where will we manage to write everything? You have already talked about so many things. You certainly have been busy lately. . . .

MOTHER: Since Christmas.

THERAPIST: Oh, yes. Now I remember getting a phone call that I didn't like at all, but I don't remember when it was.

MOTHER: Early in December.

FATHER: Yes, that was a bad moment.

THERAPIST: I'm really glad that I didn't agree to see you earlier, when things weren't going so well. I would have deprived you of the satisfaction of getting over a difficult period by your own efforts. And we would have broken an important rule: we are supposed to see each other only to talk about improvements. (*to the father*) And your mother?

FATHER: My mother. . . .

THERAPIST: Where is she living?

FATHER: At home. . . .

THERAPIST: And what about boundaries?

FATHER: I think there's been an improvement. She keeps out of things more. The credit goes to my wife, because she has learned to accept her the way she is.

THERAPIST: What else is new?

LAURA: Between me and Marina.

THERAPIST: What do you mean?

LAURA (*with satisfaction*): Things are all right now. We don't fight any more.

THERAPIST: How did that come about? You used to fight like cats and dogs.

LAURA: You know, sometimes I used to fight on purpose. I mean I did it because I was coming here, so I thought I should do it. But now I realize that if I fight, I do it for myself and my sister, so. . . .

THERAPIST (*to Marina*): What do you think about this?

MARINA: Laura is much nicer to me now.

THERAPIST (*smiling*): Explain that to me. Do you mean that Laura isn't bossy any more, or have you become bossier?

MARINA: Well, a little of both.

THERAPIST (*to the parents*): What has happened with your plans to move to Teramo?

FATHER: The plan still exists, but. . . .

MOTHER: We have to get ready for it, because I would be alone with the children all day, and if certain relationships don't improve. . . .

THERAPIST: They still need improvement. You are worried about having all the responsibility for the children, right?

MOTHER: Certainly.

LAURA (*catching on immediately*): Should I write down the improvements we have already made, or the ones we still have to work out?

THERAPIST: Here's what you can do. Divide the blackboard in half. In the upper part you can write the things you have already done, and below, give us a program that we can talk about at our next meeting five months from now, before the summer.

It is the family itself that indicates how to carry on. As often happens, it is Laura, the identified patient, who points the way to further progress. The blackboard records the family's achievements on the one hand and its new goals on the other.

By setting a date several months away for the next session, the family feels that the therapeutic system still exists. But at this point, the family has become its own therapist, and has much less need of an external guide.

Tasks Utilizing Symptoms

Utilization of the symptomatic component for a therapeutic program can be carried out in the form of either direct attack or alliance. The following will help to explain what this means.

Tasks of Attack on the Symptom

Monica, age 24, was diagnosed 10 months ago as schizophrenic. She has been hospitalized only once and has not yet been definitively assigned to a mental hospital "career." The girl shows interest in the session, although she verbally denies this. She demands an absolutely central position for herself, and at times uses her "deliria" to obtain it.

The girl's father, mother, older sister, and 17-year-old brother also participate in the session.

The family members speak in general terms about the gravity of Monica's behavior. They seem to be asking the therapist to confirm officially the need to hospitalize Monica again, even though the objective situation does not seem particularly dramatic.[4] The therapist ignores Monica's provocations (which lend support to the family's opinion about her by accentuating her "strangeness" during the session). He implicitly indicates to Monica that she cannot obtain a central position in therapy by using symptomatic behavior. He then directs a request to all family members:

THERAPIST: I would like each of you to tell me, in concrete terms, what is so serious about Monica's behavior.

MOTHER: The thing that's serious about Monica is that if she keeps on this way, she might go . . . raving mad.

THERAPIST: What you say is not exactly clear. If she goes on in what way?

MOTHER: She goes around with her hair looking so frightful. She might go over to the people next door with her hair in that mess, that would be just like her. . . .

MONICA (*standing up and putting her hands on her head*): I'm tired, I want to leave. . . .

THERAPIST: You lost a lot of rest today,[5] Monica (*the therapist leaves the room and returns with several cushions*), so I think you should rest . . . go ahead, lie down.

MONICA: What are you talking about? . . . *You* lie down. . . .

THERAPIST: I think it's important for you to rest . . . I really don't see why . . . but do as you wish . . . (*He sits down and turns toward the mother.*) Do you know your daughter well?

MOTHER: I think I do, even though. . . .

---

[4]Mental health workers must frequently deal with families who want the therapist to sanction a decision they have already made. The family hopes thereby to relieve itself of the guilt it experiences about this decision.

[5]Lately, Monica has spent several hours a day lying on her bed. Her family views this behavior with great consternation.

THERAPIST: All right, then I would like you to pretend to be Monica for a moment, and I want you to show me what Monica is like when she goes mad.

MOTHER(*reluctantly*): Monica pulls her hair down. . . .

THERAPIST: Show me how she does it.

At this point, the mother lets her hair down and acts out the imaginary situation with the next-door neighbor. The father observes with an air of detachment, while the children, including Monica, seem barely able to restrain their hilarity.

This brief excerpt demonstrates what we mean by *attacking* or *challenging the symptom*.

The symptomatic behavior of the identified patient is confronted and made to appear ridiculous by accentuating or anticipating it. In the sequence dealing with Monica's tiredness, her "differentness" is emphasized by the therapist. When the mother states that she fears that her daughter will lose her sanity, the therapist attacks the way in which the family, and particularly the mother, deals with the symptom.

One rule should always be observed. While attacking the symptomatic behavior and the manipulatory power that goes with it, we simultaneously look for areas of autonomy to protect and strengthen. The therapist can do this by modifying the symptom's interactional significance.

In the case we have cited, this twofold approach proved incisive and was accepted by the family and the identified patient. Indeed, toward the end of the session I have described, Monica was already beginning to behave more appropriately and to participate more fully, thereby expressing her confidence in the therapist.

Tasks of Alliance with the Symptom

Tasks of alliance with the symptom are particularly useful with families with preadolescent or adolescent children in the process of *achieving autonomy and separation from the family*. This process involves the family system in a situation of transformation and constitutes one of the most delicate phases in its life cycle.

We frequently observe the appearance of symptoms whose function is to keep the preadolescent or adolescent at home, just at an age at which he or she would normally be creating larger areas of individual autonomy and social participation. The request for therapy may be motivated by the appearance of phobias, tics, or disturbances in nutrition (anorexia or obesity) or by a return to enuretic or encopretic behavior. In these cases, it often proves useful to enter into an alliance with the child and to encourage the *disturbed behavior* in an effort to modify its relational significance. Bed-wetting, a tic, or even anorexia can become part of an agreement with the therapist: then these symptoms will no longer be acted out as a means of manifesting a hostile, dependent, or protective relationship toward a parent or a sibling.

The therapist can use one of several methods to attain this scope. Whatever method he chooses, he is intervening on two levels. On one hand, he provokes the child about his symptomatic behavior; on the other hand, he supports his adolescent potential. The therapist is able to promote a process of change through the interplay of these two related levels.

The case of Carla, a 14-year-old girl, may serve as an example. Carla, an only child, has reverted to bed-wetting for almost a year. Her parents are extremely upset and worried about this behavior. Carla does not present other problems; in fact, her parents are lavish with praise for her scholastic achievements and her general common sense. The girl fulfills all of their expectations. If it were not for this problem of her enuresis, which clearly limits her freedom of action, "everything would be going smoothly."

After a few sessions, it is clear that her enuresis keeps her parents at once united and divided, and that Carla's common sense consists in limiting her own autonomy in order to protect them. Her mother is able to conceal her own disillusionment by dedicating herself completely to helping her daughter to overcome the problem. She has resorted to rubber underpants, a waterproof mattress cover, and other similar devices. A great deal of her time and thought are devoted to worrying about Carla's bed-wetting problem. The father plays an apparently neutral role. When asked his opinion about the problem, he tends to minimize it or to criticize—politely but decisively—his wife's way of educating Carla. Carla says that she is sorry, not for herself (she can still keep up her friendships without revealing her problem), but "for my mother, who suffers so much over it, and for my father, who gets into a bad mood because of her."

It seems as though all three have found in Carla's enuresis a method that, even though it is dysfunctional in terms of the utilization of energy, permits them to preserve the family's homeostasis. That is, a balance is maintained in which interpersonal tensions are not allowed to reach an unacceptable level of intensity, and spouse conflicts can be expressed indirectly through the problem of Carla. Protecting Carla becomes a means of keeping her inside the system. If Carla becomes more independent, the spouses will be forced to confront one another and the outside world directly.

For Carla, protecting her parents (this is obviously denied by all three) represents a way of remaining inside the system and of avoiding the search for areas of greater autonomy and responsibility appropriate to her age.

To change this situation, the vicious circle of protectiveness must be broken. As a first move, we attempt to encourage Carla's rebelliousness. We predict that the parents' protective attitude will change to resentment. With this in mind, the therapist divides the family in the sessions, holding individual meetings with Carla. He proposes to Carla that they work together on the problem of her enuresis, but on condition that their work remain a secret between them. Carla is to keep a daily diary (which she must bring with her to the therapeutic sessions). She is instructed to keep it hidden from her parents. In it she is asked to note frequency, quantity, and time for her enuretic behavior, as well as the quantity and kinds of liquids she consumes after five o'clock in the afternoon. If during a night she does not wet her bed, she must describe everything that happened during the preceding day. The therapist justifies his request by explaining to her that they need a precise picture of the situation in order to find a solution and that any effort on his part will fail if she does not cooperate.

This *task of alliance with the symptom* has several objectives. First, it is intended to create a close bond between the therapist and the girl. This bond is initially based on the symptom, whose affective connotation has been modified. Since the symptom is no longer enacted for the family, it becomes a pretext for creating a pact with an important adult, thereby utilizing Carla's adolescent potential constructively. Her capacities will gradually find new and more adequate outlets.

By giving considerable attention to Carla's enuresis, both during the sessions and in the task assigned as "homework," the therapist tries to desensitize this area, and at the same time, he encourages Carla to rebel against him. As Carla is gradually led to feel that she is valued for her adolescent capacities, she will begin to feel more reluctant to talk about bed-wetting. However, it will be possible to reduce the attention given to this subject and to move on to subjects concerning more mature forms of competence only when the symptom really loses its original significance.

No definitive solution to the problem can be found without simultaneously producing changes at the level of the parents, who have until now felt a strong need to keep Carla between them. The first phase of therapy might consist in provoking in the parents a resentful rather than a protective attitude toward Carla's symptom. In this case, Carla would be more likely to rebel.

By instructing the parents to exercise greater control over Carla's enuresis, Carla's task will be more difficult. She will have to exert herself to exclude her parents from the dynamics of bed-wetting. For the parents, and particularly for the mother, Carla's secretiveness will come as an unpleasant surprise; enuresis will no longer serve as a vehicle for protective interaction and will instead become grounds for confrontation and dispute.

Once the reality of Carla's adolescence has been accepted by all, including Carla herself, the therapist's intervention will shift to the real problems of the family. His work will be facilitated once the family no longer requires a patient to mask these problems.

PARADOXICAL TASKS

In order to understand what a paradoxical intervention is, we must first define what we mean by *paradox* and illustrate the effects it has on human interaction.[6]

We may define as paradoxical a situation in which an affirmation is true if, and only if, it is false. A situation of this kind arises when two messages that are pragmatically incompatible are transmitted simultaneously.

Paradoxes are used frequently in human behavior, although they often pass unrecognized. Our daily life as parents, wives, husbands, children, friends, employees, employers, etc., is permeated with paradoxical communications, which appear in very varied forms.

[6]An attempt to formulate a theoretical definition can be found in Watzlawick *et al.* (1967), Chapter 5.

Many important effects of paradox on human interaction have been studied by Bateson, Jackson, Haley, and Weakland (1956) in connection with families with schizophrenic patterns of interaction. It was they who first identified certain kinds of interactions from which the term *double bind*[7] was drawn.

The double bind was later described by Sluzki and Verón (1971) as a *universal theory of pathogenesis*, that is, not as a theory applicable only to schizophrenic transactions, but of general applicability.

There is no doubt that if we analyze the interactions between persons who are bound to each other in close relationships—for example, families, communes, work groups, political or religious groups, institutions—we find that in one way or another all of us are exposed to double-bind situations. The difference lies in the fact that many of these experiences are probably isolated or incomplete, even though they may have a traumatic effect. For example, many *crisis* situations are in fact responses to *paradoxical situations*.

Very different effects are produced when a person is exposed to a double bind for a prolonged period of time. Little by little, he adapts himself to it until he finally considers it the only available model of communication and he becomes an active participant in an endless game.[8] A situation of this kind produces not an isolated trauma but a pathological model of interaction that proves extremely difficult to change and that eventually traps the participants in a vicious circle.

The Significance of Paradox in Therapy

In psychotherapy, the use of paradox arises in a different framework. It does not force the patient to react with a pathological response; instead it interrupts a vicious circle.

---

[7]The "ingredients" of a double bind can be summarized in the following way: (1) the existence of an intense relationship having high physical and psychological value between two or more persons (family life, economic dependence, imprisonment, faith in a cause or an ideology, psychotherapy, etc.); (2) The sending of a message structured in such a way that (a) it affirms something, (b) it affirms something concerning its own affirmation; (c) these two affirmations are mutually contradictory. For example, if the message is a command, the command must be disobeyed in order to be obeyed. In this way it is impossible to determine the meaning of the message. (3) The receiver cannot escape from the frame of reference established by the paradoxical message, and it is therefore impossible for him to give an *adequate* response.

[8]An endless game is an irreversible situation in which the participants are unable, even if they wish to do so, to change the rules of the relationship that have set the game in motion.

The use of therapeutic paradoxes is motivated by the fact that many families request help but at the same time seem to reject all offers of help. The therapist is thereby drawn into a *game* in which every effort on his part to act as an agent of change is nullified by the family group. In systemic terms, these apparently contradictory attitudes derive from the dynamic equilibrium existing between opposite and interacting forces: the tendency toward change, which is implicit in the request for help, and the preponderant tendency toward homeostasis[9], which leads the family to repeat its habitual behavioral sequences.[10] The coexistence of these forces can easily entangle the therapist in the family's contradictory logic of *"help me to change, but without changing anything."*

In this way, the therapist finds himself caught in a kind of double bind. Every effort he makes to change something will be boycotted on some levels, while on other levels the family will continue to ask for his help.[11]

Instead of persisting in a futile effort to promote change, the therapist can *accept* (rather than submit to) the contradiction[12] that he is faced with. This enables him to stimulate the tendencies toward change present at other levels in the family system. That is, by accepting the "double bind," he puts himself into a position that is exactly the opposite of what the family expects of him. His response to the family's paradoxical request is a counterparadox (Selvini *et al.*, 1978) because it creates the contradictory communication typical of the double bind.[13]

---

[9]In this part of the book, I am keeping the concepts of *homeostasis* and *change* rigidly separated in order to present the material as clearly as possible. In reality, these terms cannot be distinguished so easily, nor can they be subjected to moral judgments that identify homeostasis with the negative aspects of the system and change with the positive aspects. Therapists often arbitrarily make value judgments of this kind when they try to define the relationship between the therapeutic system and the family system. Almost automatically, the therapist is tempted to consider the tendency toward change "better," because it corresponds with his goals. In reality, tendencies toward change are neither "better" nor "worse" than homeostatic tendencies.

[10]The reader should keep in mind that these habitual behavior sequences have a *communicational* significance among the various family members and between the family system and the therapist.

[11]In therapy, the family resorts to the model of communication used in its most important relationships, where each member denies or boycotts at one level what it appears to encourage at another level.

[12]By consciously accepting the contradiction, the therapist is able to avoid becoming involved in this unproductive kind of situation.

[13]The therapist is able to create a counterparadoxical position only after he has established an intense relationship with the other family members, if they are present. Moreover, his *power* in the therapeutic system must be real and continuous.

He can obtain this result by prescribing the *symptom* to the identified patient[14] and by prescribing its own dysfunctional rules to the family system.

Prescribing the Symptom

One way of using paradox is *to prescribe the symptom*. Here paradox is used as a therapeutic response to the "help me change without changing anything" reasoning that has immobilized the identified patient or the entire family system.[15] If the patient turns to the therapist requesting help, the therapist advises him that in order to get well he should continue to use the "disturbed behavior."

The technique, known as *prescribing the symptom*, has probably been used intuitively by psychiatrists for a long time. In 1928, Dunlop wrote about *negative suggestion*: his method consisted in provoking the patient by instructing him not to do a certain thing in order to stimulate him to do just that thing.[16] More recently, Frankl (1957) has described another provocative form of intervention, called *paradoxical intention*, which he has used extensively with phobic and obsessive patients. His method is really based on prescribing the phobic symptom, thereby bringing the patient to anticipate it and to exaggerate its intensity. This technique eventually produces a change in the nature of the symptom itself: the symptom begins to create less anxiety, and in some cases the patient

[14]We will see later how prescribing the symptom affects family rules as well. It is essential that the therapist evaluate this aspect of his intervention.

[15]"We would like to emphasize that it is impossible to create a model of observation and interactional intervention merely by including all members of a family in therapy, instead of only the identified patient. The presence of the other members merely offers the opportunity (to a therapist capable of utilizing it in interactional terms) to directly activate interactions among the single components and subsystems, so that the therapist and the family can evaluate and verify the multiple feedback that emerges. But the presence of the family group does not *ipso facto* guarantee a correct interactional approach. In fact, the context of accusation that often arises when the therapist tries to present himself as *apparently neutral* (in accordance with the medical-psychiatric model) may induce the therapist to fall back on a linear model in evaluating the situation. On the other hand, individual therapist-patient sessions do not automatically exclude an interactional approach, although they do limit the therapist's ability to activate and verify directly certain modalities of interaction between the patient and other significant people (Andolfi & Menghi, 1976a).

[16]It is easy to introduce this mode of intervention, but it is difficult to control it over a period of time. In our clinical experience, it has proved particularly useful with adolescents when the degree of provocation by the therapist has been judiciously calculated to turn the rebellious tendencies typical of this age group to constructive uses.

begins to see it as ridiculous. The result is that the patient gradually succeeds in placing some degree of distance between himself and his neurotic behavior.

In his psychotherapeutic work with schizophrenics, Rosen (1953) has proposed another similar technique, which he calls *direct analysis*. Rosen gives his patients paradoxical instructions, entailing a massive resumption of symptomatic behavior, when the patient is on the verge of a real relapse. By prescribing a worsening of his situation, Rosen prevents it from occurring. The therapist's intervention gives the patient a greater awareness of his disturbances. According to Rosen, if the patient is able to increase his symptomatic behavior at will, he is probably able to control it as well.

Another similar technique described by Don D. Jackson (1963), used with patients with *paranoid traits*, consists in teaching them to become more suspicious. Haley (1976), utilizing Milton Erikson's observations, has demonstrated how paradoxical directives play a fundamental role in hypnosis. In hypnosis,

> Two levels of message are simultaneously being communicated by the hypnotist: he is saying 'Do as I say' and within that framework he is saying 'Don't do as I say, behave spontaneously.' The way the subject adapts to such a conflicting set of directives is to undergo a change and behave in a way described as trance behavior.

We frequently use prescription of the symptom as part of a broader paradoxical strategy intended to unbalance very rigid family systems. We can take a family with an anorectic girl as an example. The daughter, who is the identified patient, controls all of the communication that takes place in the family group. The parents abdicate all authority to her, and it is she who defines all family relations, including the marital relationship. By prescribing the symptom (refusal to eat) in the session, we can provoke reversals in the system because now the symptom, usually utilized by the patient to control the relationship, becomes involuntary. The prescription is given during a lunch session in which the therapist and the other members of the family eat normally, while the daughter is *forbidden* to eat.

Since the girl's refusal to eat is now involuntary, it no longer serves as a means for controlling the family's interactions. At the same time, the parents can no longer use incongruent messages like "Eat, but don't eat." The prescription therefore interrupts the family game based on the girl's eating problem. It also helps to expose the rules of the anorectic system, thereby facilitating the formation of a valid therapeutic system.

What M. Erikson referred to as "encouraging a relapse" may also be considered a paradoxical intervention. When a therapist thinks that a patient is going to have a relapse, or when he shows an improvement that seems unstable, or in cases in which symptomatic behavior is used in a particularly manipulative way by the patient (and by the other family members), Erikson suggested that the therapist predict and encourage a relapse—in order to prevent its occurrence. By using this strategy, the therapist paradoxically offers the patient alternative choices of behavior by denying to him that he has any autonomous choice. The more the therapist denies this autonomy, the more the patient tries to achieve it.

In our own work, we use the technique of prescribing the symptom whenever we feel that it may effectively interrupt redundant behavior and thereby give us the possibility of joining the interactional world of the patient, even though the other significant members of the family may be absent.

Prescribing the symptom to an individual patient does not in itself resolve a situation of distress. It constitutes a tactical move whose aim is to create openings in particularly rigid systems so that latent potentialities can be expressed.

It is important to note that the patient's attitude of *I don't want to change* often expresses his rejection of the idea that "someone" can change something. The message that he transmits to the therapist may be *I don't want "you" to change something in me.* In other words, the patient may be trying to reproduce in the therapeutic situation the same exasperated symmetrical tension that exists in his intrafamilial relationships, where no one can accept any redefinition concerning himself, and where each family member tries to impose his own redefinition on the others (Selvini et al., 1978).

By utilizing this kind of symmetrical relationship, the therapist can expect the patient to initiate some kind of change—in order to prove that the therapist was wrong.

For example, if a therapist accepts a depressed patient's behavior without trying to mitigate it or belittle its importance, and instead encourages the patient to express his despair more freely, he can produce a series of effects. To begin with, the patient may feel more "understood" and he will not need to resist the therapist in order to prove that he is wrongly underestimating the problem. Any effort to console a depressed person by telling him, "Things aren't as bad as they seem; you'll see, everything will be all right," usually has the effect of increasing the person's state of dejection. If, on the contrary, the therapist exaggerates the patient's own definition of his depressed state, if he encourages and prescribes the patient's tendency to refuse change, then the patient is forced to "correct" the "erroneous" view of the therapist by demonstrating that he is not so severely depressed.

Prescribing the Rules

In family therapy we also use the paradoxical technique of consistently applying the rigid, dysfunctional family rules that maintain the system's homeostasis. This technique makes it possible to transform the system by provoking infractions of the rules that have led to the problem and that maintain it.

To clarify what we mean by prescribing the rules, we can start with two hypotheses:

1. In every family system, as in any other system, there exists a dynamic equilibrium between a homeostatic tendency (which we will call H) and a tendency toward transformation (which we will call T).

2. The therapeutic system, by definition, seeks to promote change[17] in dysfunctional family groups that are usually characterized by a marked prevalence of homeostatic tendencies. When the therapeutic system activates a family system in which the T forces have already been liberated and are available for utilization (that is, when the tendency to maintain a rigid homeostasis is not dominant), then the two Ts can be easily integrated and will reciprocally reinforce each other, leading to a rapid resolution of the problem. (This occurs, for example, in certain acute crisis situations that create instability and set the system in motion.)

On the other hand, when the T present in the therapeutic system sets in motion a family system in which the tendency toward T has been suffocated by a *rigid set of internal rules,* the therapeutic T will be be seen as a threat and it will eventually be neutralized by the family's homeostatic forces.[18] The therapist finds himself in a paradoxical position similar to the one that locks the family members in a double bind: *I would like*

---

[17]The most basic change consists in establishing a new equilibrium between H and T.

[18]Family homeostasis has a pathological connotation only when it is excessively rigid. Even the tendency to change, when it is incompatible with all efforts to reestablish any kind of homeostasis, becomes a dysfunctional form of interaction.

to change, but I can't; why don't you help me to change without changing anything? [19]

In cases where the therapeutic T is threatening[20] to the family, the therapist can still encourage change by disguising his T as H, thus reinforcing the H of the family system by prescribing it or suggesting ways of strengthening it. This is one way of responding to the family's paradoxical position of *help me, but don't help me.* That is, the therapist can respond with a counterparadox: All right, *I will help you by not helping you.* In this way, he confirms the rigidity of the family's homeostasis. The family cannot oppose the T of the therapist because it has been formulated so as to appear synonymous with the family's H. The family is forced to change—that is, to liberate its own T—in order to prove to the therapist that he is making a mistake by confirming the family's tendency to resist change.

This strategy attempts to substitute *a new game* for the *endless game* played by the family in the past. By denying the possibility of alternative behavior, the therapist acts in a way that is at once provocative and liberating. His approach enables the family group to respond with a therapeutic counterprovocation (*I'll prove to you that you are wrong*). Over and beyond the interactional message that it contains, the counterprovocation permits the family to try out new ways of relating and solving the problem.

Since the therapist's intervention is perceived by the family as a challenge, the family feels itself relieved of a part of the responsibility that initially weighed upon it—that is, the responsibility implicit in *changing only for oneself* (and not for someone else, particularly for the person whose task it is to stimulate change). *To change for the therapist* (which means demonstrating that he is wrong) signifies entering into a new state of abnormality. In many cases, however, a transitional phase of this kind is necessary. It helps the family members to free themselves from a severely disturbed reality so that they can develop more acceptable interactional patterns without resorting to scapegoating.

---

[19]"Without changing anything" is the final phrase of a complex message: "In order to help me to change, you should be what someone else should have been but was not" (Selvini *et al.*, 1978).

[20]In rigidly calibrated systems such as families with schizophrenic members, every change is experienced as a danger, a threat. This is true whether the stimulus to the family to change comes from the outside (in the form of social, political, or cultural pressure) or from within the system itself (in the form of the birth, death, or departure of a member; the adolescent crisis of a child, etc.). The system reacts negatively to such changes and becomes even more rigid (Selvini *et al.*, 1978).

The family has to decide whether to carry out the therapist's directives (which implies accepting the therapist's power) or whether to defy these directives (which signifies changing the rules). Moreover, the family members perceive (whether or not they follow the therapist's directives) that the real game, of which they are both protagonists and prisoners, has become explicit and that their habitual patterns of relating are becoming less effective.

I would like to discuss one more aspect of the relationship that is formed between the therapeutic system and the family system. In this situation, the family system sets into motion its most rigid homeostatic tendencies. It will probably act out these tendencies for the therapist in the most ostentatious way possible, as though to test the therapist's ability. By acting out its homeostatic tendencies, the family system shows the therapist what direction to take,[21] and at the same time it evaluates his credibility and dependability by forcing him to deal with rigid family rules. Our experience has taught us to expect a considerable increase in confidence and cooperation on the part of the family if the therapist succeeds in discovering the family's games without getting caught up in them.

The following are a few examples of what we have discussed. The first concerns the case of a couple whom we had in therapy for about three months. Therapy was requested because of the husband's "alcoholism." This definition of the problem was offered by the wife and was implicitly accepted by the husband, who accused his wife of being the principal cause of his drinking. After a few sessions, the dynamics of his problem, in relational terms, seemed to be as follows.

Neither husband nor wife were willing to specify the extent of his drinking. This led us to suspect that there was some sort of complicity concerning the problem that served to maintain a certain level of equilibrium in the system. He almost never drank at home, but his wife frequently "discovered" him drinking at a bar. He seemed to arrange things so that his wife would catch him and then "reproach" him. For example, he took their young son to the bar with him; the son then told his mother or his mother's friends what he had seen. (The wife's father had died of cirrhosis of the liver; it seemed clear that drinking had special significance for her.) The wife aggravated the problem by attempting to control her husband. For example, she insisted on smelling his breath

---

[21]The identified patient often implicitly expresses contradictions existing in the family and sometimes indicates ways of overcoming these contradictions.

when he came home and refused to have sexual intercourse with him because of his "vices." Her efforts enraged him, and he retreated into nostalgic reminiscences of the good old times before their marriage. He would then drink "for consolation," leaving evidence that his wife would be sure to discover.

If we had used any of these units of information in a linear way, without considering the other units and the circular relation that existed between them, we would have run a series of risks. First of all, we would have risked being sucked into the rules of an endless game[22]; second, we would have been tempted to take sides on the contents of the issue as presented by the husband or the wife and to enter into an alliance that would have unbalanced the system and placed the blame on the excluded spouse.

These considerations convinced us to use a paradoxical intervention to provoke a change in the couple's rules—which they seemed incapable of doing by themselves. We predicted that a therapeutic paradox—prescribing the very rules that had set in motion the couple's game—would facilitate a change in the couple's rules about interacting. In other words, we wanted *to promote change by directing them not to change.* By instructing each spouse to supervise the other, we hoped to prevent the possibility of reciprocal control. This maneuver could succeed only after the therapist had gained power and control over the entire sequence of interactions in the couple-therapist relationship.

The prescription was formulated in the following manner. The wife was instructed to increase supervision over her husband and not to miss any occasion for "catching him in the act." We told her to allow her husband to consume daily a set quantity of alcohol (large enough so that her husband could not easily exceed it), which she should administer to her husband herself, if necessary by going with him to the bar. We explained to her that this would relieve her of her anxiety about having a "depraved" husband who was drowning himself in rivers of alcohol in some bar in Rome. In this way, she could gain total control of the situation. At the same time, she was told to uphold her own "moral principles" and to abstain from sexual intercourse with her husband when he smelled of alcohol.

---

[22]"Each sees himself as responding to the other but never also as a stimulus to the other's actions. They do not see the full nature of their game, its true circularity. These discrepant views become material for further symmetrical escalation" (Watzlawick, Beavin, & Jackson, 1967, p. 180).

The husband, in turn, was instructed to check up assiduously on his wife to be sure that she would not try to cheat him by increasing or diminishing the agreed-upon daily dosage of alcohol. Any failure on the wife's part would clearly indicate her bad faith and her unwillingness to help find a solution to the problem. He was also asked to be sure that his wife made absolutely no sexual requests when he smelled of alcohol.[23]

Formulated in these terms, the task was presented to the couple. They seemed interested in collaborating in a concrete task that promised to help them to escape from a situation of exasperation and continual resentment. The therapist advised the couple that they would probably meet with difficulties in carrying out the task and, in particular, he warned them that it would be extremely difficult to keep each other's behavior under complete control.

The following week, the couple reported back to the therapist about what had happened. The wife had gone to the bar with her husband, but not as often as planned. As soon as she started accompanying him, her anxiety about drinking vanished. The husband seemed proud of his wife for her courage in accompanying him (it was the first time in their married life that she had done this), and he verbalized his satisfaction. The husband, too, had been only partially successful in controlling his wife. During the session, we learned that on some occasions it had been the husband who refused to go to the bar with her because "he didn't feel like drinking." The wife had also made sexual advances, ignoring the prohibition that was part of her assigned task. He told us that he was very pleased by her unexpected demonstrations of affection.

The therapist responded to the couple's account by saying that although he had foreseen that they would fail to carry out such a difficult task, he had not predicted so complete a failure. He alerted them to the danger that by sabotaging the task in this way, they were demonstrating their refusal to overcome their marital problems. He then reassigned the

---

[23]Paradoxical tasks are tasks in which details are formulated in an intentionally obsessive way and certain habitual behaviors are purposely exaggerated. They take on bizarre characteristics that can create problems for an inexperienced therapist. A therapist lacking sufficient experience may assign tasks without having the necessary conviction, because he is eager to establish credibility with the family (and with himself). His insecurity will be perceived by the family and the family system will utilize it, thus reducing the tasks's effectiveness. I would like to emphasize that the therapist must achieve sufficient emotional distance from the situation to conduct a paradoxical intervention. His intervention must be based on an accurate and objective analysis of the underlying significance of the messages and the relationships that he observes.

same task, underlining certain aspects and asking each spouse to bring to the following session a written record concerning any "transgressions" made by the other.[24]

As a result of this paradoxical intervention, the spouses united in a renewed effort to sabotage the task assigned by the therapist. Consequently the husband's alcohol problem, which until then had seemed unsolvable, disappeared. The couple was then able to reactivate the more positive potentialities of their relationship.

In this case, the paradox consisted in *prescribing the dysfunctional rules* of the couple. It produced a liberating effect on both spouses, for once they succeeded in abandoning their endless game, they were able to discover new ways of relating.

I would like to present another example of prescribing the rules, this time to an entire family group. In the following case, family therapy served to avoid hospitalization[25] for Renzo (age 14) and gave the family confidence in its ability to solve its own problems.

In the sixth session, the rules of the spouse relationship are explored. By now, the family no longer thinks it necessary to hospitalize their son. By activating the relations between subsystems, the therapist has brought to light the redundancies that are maintaining some of the family's interactional problems. These can be summarized as follows:

1. When the parents talk to each other, they talk almost exclusively about Renzo, and only about his problems.

2. Renzo systematically activates his parents in such a way as to make them continue to worry about him. He is always positioned between his parents.

3. Renzo continually draws attention to his parents' responsibility for his fear of being "mentally ill." He tells us that he has searched in the psychology columns of newspapers for information that would diminish his fears.

4. If either of the parents irritates Renzo, Renzo hits his younger brother.

5. Renzo makes his mother find excuses so that he can avoid his companions. This behavior is syntonic with the mother's need to control her son.

---

[24]When the family first begins to change, it is useful to reinforce the task. By denying that change is occurring, the therapist forces the family to reinforce it.

[25]Renzo was brought in by his parents for consultation. They had previously been advised to hospitalize their son "for observation": he had been diagnosed as having a character neurosis and paranoid traits.

Shortly before the end of the session, the therapist distributes a sheet of paper to each family member and dictates the task:

1. The mother must answer all telephone calls. All calls for Renzo should be answered with excuses to make sure that he doesn't go out "too much." If Renzo disobeys this rule in any way, the mother should make a note of it in a special notebook to be kept for this purpose. If she breaks the rule, then Renzo should make note of it.

2. Every time Renzo gets angry at his father and mother, he should "get it off his chest" by getting mad at his younger brother. The younger brother must note in writing every time that Renzo fails to obey this rule. At this point, Renzo asks whether it might not be better for him not to get mad at anyone. The therapist cuts short his interruption, without answering, and continues.

3. The father must go to a library with Renzo to look up information on character neuroses. The results of their research should be written down and brought to the next session.

The central problem is the adolescent son's need to achieve autonomy and the difficulties that this process is creating in his family. The therapist has "packaged" a series of directives based on material brought in by the family members. The common denominator of these directives is that they all aim at establishing control by each member over the other members. In fact, a system of reciprocal controls is one of the elements in the family system that most seriously limits the autonomy of the identified patient and of the other members. In particular, the first task accepts and reinforces the rule of reciprocal control between mother and son (this rule also implies a coalition against the father). The motivation for this task given by the therapist—"so that he won't go out too much"—is really a stimulus for the boy and a challenge to his unrealized adolescent potential.

The second task makes Renzo's blackmailing of his parents appear ridiculous and absurd. Renzo avoids confronting them directly (the parents' attitude reinforces his behavior); he prefers to play the part of a crazy irresponsible child rather than assume a more adult role, which he fears. But the task underlines the intentional aspect of his bizarre behavior. It thereby unmasks his game and makes it seem infantile and useless. Moreover, with the younger brother supervising how he implements the task, his mode of behavior—previously in some way accepted as the inevitable result of his "character neurosis"—will become progressively less justifiable.

The third task differs from the first two. Although like the others it is intended to emphasize Renzo's disturbance, it introduces an important variation: it aims at dismantling the myth of "character neurosis" (which has paralyzed the entire family) by making it a subject for intellectual research and analysis. This task will also yield information concerning the ability of the system to accept a more direct relationship between Renzo and his father. This variation in the family's usual transactional pattern temporarily excludes the mother from the father-son relationship. By excluding the mother, the therapist is not seconding an existing family rule; rather, he is exploring the system's ability to redistribute relationships and alliances. The fact that it is "too" early in therapy to introduce an "excessively" countersystemic move is precisely what provokes a series of lively counterreactions on the part of the family; these will be extremely useful in guiding successive interventions.

As for the other directives given by the therapist, the family soon experiences difficulty in behaving according to its habitual interactional models and finds it necessary to look for alternative ways of relating.

The following transcription is from a session held with a family with a 21-year-old daughter, Anna, who presented the kind of behavior usually defined as schizophrenic. The case was extremely difficult because of the particular type of interactions common to this kind of family group. In the preceding session, it had seemed to us that Anna's behavior fulfilled a protective function vis-à-vis the rest of the family and toward the parents in particular. In this session, Anna's absence seemed to confirm this hypothesis. The family members all felt free to talk about her, and for her. It was clear that she was the source of great concern to all of them.

THERAPIST: I would like each of you to telephone Anna and ask whether she is willing to come to the next session.

FATHER: I'm very pessimistic. (*The mother shakes her head with a dejected expression of resignation. The brother and sister are also pessimistic. A telephone is brought into the room. Each member of the family in turn asks Anna if she is willing to come, and each time Anna replies that the problem does not concern her.*)

THERAPIST (*the therapist comes to the telephone and talks to Anna*): . . . Well, if you don't want to come, there is no reason to insist. Listen, Anna, now I want to ask your family something. I would like you to listen, but without saying anything. (*To the other family members*) I would like each of you to answer me, holding the receiver in your hand and speaking into this microphone. I am going to lay down a rule: you are not to speak to Anna—you must speak only to me. This is the question: What is the problem in this family? (*The family members take turns answering the question into the receiver and Anna listens without replying. The first attempt of the mother to elicit a reply from her daughter is immediately blocked by the therapist. There are no further attempts to break the rule. After the family members have spoken, the therapist comes to the phone and puts the same question to Anna.*)[26]

THERAPIST: Anna, in ten minutes I would like to ask you and your family another question. Can you please call us back?

ANNA: Yes.

THERAPIST: All right, I'll give you the number . . . so long.

In this phase of therapy, the therapist is making *exploratory* moves to sound out his relationship with Anna and to establish a basis for negotiating with her. This information will help the therapist to join the family system. Exactly 10 minutes later, Anna called.

THERAPIST: Hello, Anna. I would like you to listen at first, the way you did last time. (*To the other family members*). What's wrong with Anna? (*The therapist holds out the receiver towards the others.*) Who wants to answer first?

Again, each one replied to the therapist's question, while Anna listened. Then the therapist asked Anna the same question while the others listened to her reply.

In this case, the therapist gave a paradoxical response to the delicate situation created by the absence of the identified patient.[27] The paradox consisted in directing the family not to communicate with Anna and simultaneously directing them to communicate with her, and similarly, in telling Anna not to participate in the session and yet asking her to

[26]An amplifier was put on the telephone so that everyone present could hear. Anna was informed of this.

[27]The absence of the identified patient or of another family member is not a decisive factor, nor does it paralyze progress in interactional therapy. In this particular case, the absence of the identified patient was probably the result of a "protective" maneuver by the family system and therefore did not reflect an autonomous decision on Anna's part.

participate. The therapist gave a directive and at the same time denied that he was giving it. In this way, he forced the family members to do exactly what they had indicated that they did not want to do, and at the same time, he denied that this was what was happening. Moreover, by using a series of double messages, the therapist paradoxically encouraged Anna to come to the next session, by accepting and encouraging her absence from this session.

One of the homeostatic mechanisms used by the family was circumvented by a paradoxical technique. All members of the family participated in the session by denying their presence, and messages were allowed to be transmitted by denying the communicational value of these messages. Anna did come to the following session and took an active part in the therapeutic process.

What parameters should be taken into consideration in deciding whether to utilize a *paradoxical* task or a *restructuring* task? There is no simple answer to this problem. In large part, the choice depends on the style and the personality of the therapist, who may have more skill in one kind of approach than in another. However, paradoxical tasks are more effective with families that present paradoxical attitudes and behaviors, which make it futile to intervene on a level of congruence.

It is easier to learn to repeat a given formula than to deal directly with an ongoing situation. Sometimes an evaluation of a family system is based not on that system's specific characteristics but on the therapist's lack of experience. For example, an inexperienced therapist may prefer to rely on the "magical" effect of a paradoxical task rather than on a thorough analysis of transactional patterns and on his own ability to conduct the sessions. The apparent simplicity of certain tasks and the possibility of repeating them may induce some therapists to apply ready-made formulas at the expense of his patients and their families. This way of proceding can only discredit this methodology of research and intervention, which requires serious preparation, not improvisation.

Concerning the so-called miraculous effects often attributed to paradoxical interventions, my views are not quite that optimistic. But there is no doubt that this kind of intervention is of the greatest importance in the treatment of seriously disturbed families, and particularly in families with schizophrenic transactions. Since paradoxical techniques are the most effective means of disrupting rigid interactional patterns, they are particularly useful with this kind of family system, where the gravity of the disturbance indicates the presence of powerful homeostatic forces.

A therapeutic counterparadox will not necessarily resolve a state of distress in an individual or in a family, although it can be a highly effective instrument. A counterparadox proposed by a significant person, the therapist, who is outside the family system, often successfully provokes a change in family rules when the family alone seems unable to do this.

If one reads the not very abundant literature on therapeutic paradox, it seems to be taken for granted that paradoxes are—and should be—unintelligible on all levels. Our experience leads us to believe that this is not true. Often, when an individual or a family group carries out a paradoxical task, or plans how to carry it out, they gain a more-or-less precise insight into the implicit meaning of the task. This is particularly common in therapies with adolescents in the process of achieving autonomy. These young patients easily accept the *game of provocation* inherent in the task and in the paradoxical approach, although they may discuss the details with great scrupulousness and earnestness. In this way, they in turn communicate how effective this mode of intervention is in activating change without causing family members to "lose face."

Metaphorical Tasks

Metaphor as a Means of Communication

The language of metaphor is a means of transmitting to and receiving messages from an individual, a couple, or a whole family.

Speaking and listening metaphorically enable us to send and receive multiple messages at different levels of abstraction. For example, when a therapist is listening to someone talking about a problem, he keeps in mind that on a literal level, the speaker is communicating facts or opinions, but that on an analogic level, he is communicating something that cannot be stated explicitly (Haley, 1976). When parents talk about their child's problem, the therapist can listen to each one's description on various levels; for example, as a description of the child's specific difficulties, or as a statement concerning the speaker, the other spouse, or the marital relationship. Moreover, what the speaker says about the child may implicitly refer to the therapeutic context, that is, to the relationship between the family system and the therapist.

For example, if a mother says that her son is insecure and frightened, she may mean, on another level, that her husband is insecure and frightened and that their marital relationship is precarious. If a father states that the son threatens to run away from home, it may be the wife who is threatening to leave him. If both parents describe an adolescent daughter's disorderly eating behavior, in which she oscillates between refusal of food and overeating, at another level they may be communicating that there is a lack of order in their marital relationship. Again, if the couple says that their son is violent and that they fear he will engage in delinquent behavior, it is quite possible that on an analogic level they are speaking about their own relationship and the violence of their own interpersonal transactions.

A therapist can utilize metaphor in various ways. He can speak metaphorically or he can activate the family by utilizing a metaphorical approach, in particular by assigning metaphorical tasks. Speaking metaphorically is an effective means for gathering information that would be hard to elicit in other ways from family groups that are particularly rigid and defensive. For example, it is possible to discuss an issue metaphorically by choosing a topic that is similar to the problematic situation, while avoiding explicit reference to the connection between the two.

In certain cases metaphorical communication promotes change by producing insight, at times in a dramatic way.

An example is the following case of a particularly rigid couple, with sexual difficulties and a taboo on discussion of this subject. The situation began to open up when one of the partners started to talk about his desire to repaint their bedroom. This theme, which was introduced as further proof of the inability of the couple to reach an agreement, was utilized metaphorically by the therapist to promote change in their sexual relationship. He requested husband and wife to describe the size and shape of the room, the furniture and how it was arranged, the color of the walls, the lighting, and other details of this kind. Both partners replied with such vivacity that the therapist decided to continue probing in this direction. On the supposition that the subject contained analogies to their sexual problem, the therapist made use of the discussion without making the correlation evident. To avoid arousing the couple's defenses, he simple asked each one how he would have liked to have the room repainted, what was the spouse's favorite color, who would have mixed the paint, and who would have done the actual painting. He also asked what clothes they would have worn to paint in and how they thought they could collaborate in this job. Finally, he instructed them to start work on the room the following weekend when they would be free and relaxed. At the following session, they were to describe how the project had been carried out and which initiatives on the part of each spouse had pleased the other during their work.

The task worked out very well. The couple came to the next session extremely pleased because they had accomplished something concrete that they both desired. They related that while working, they had both experienced irresistible sexual desires and had found renewed pleasure in being together. This automatically led to a discussion of their sexual problems without any direct solicitation by the therapist. It also created a new atmosphere in the sessions because they had experienced in a gratifying way the possibility of modifying their habitual way of relating.

Another way of communicating with metaphors is to attribute to some object emotional connotations that are appropriate to an individual or to an interpersonal relationship. For example, a chair left vacant by one of the family members can be used to personify the absent person. The therapist himself may speak or he can invite someone else to communicate his feelings to the chair. Or he can ask the siblings of the identified patient to take turns sitting in the identified patient's chair and play his role. The therapist can offer a doll to be held on the lap of an overprotective mother of a grown-up child, and she can be questioned about her need to hold "someone" in her arms. Finally, members can be asked to talk to their father's briefcase instead of to the father "who is never there." An adolescent boy, who was an only child, was not progressing toward emancipation. He had taken over the leadership of the family, while the parents played a subordinate role. He was asked to invent a puppet show: he was to play the role of the puppet master, while the parents were to maneuver the puppets and speak for them, following the script invented by the son.

The metaphorical utilization of emotively charged objects has proved extremely useful in rigid family systems where it can be futile or even harmful to activate verbal channels of communication.

Using Metaphorical Tasks

Giving directives in therapy is one way of promoting change, but there are many people who are unwilling to follow instructions even though they may acknowledge their usefulness. Some people are more willing to accept tasks if they do not consciously recognize them as such,[28] or if the task does not directly involve the problem situation.

Metaphorical prescriptions function well in such cases. If a therapist thinks it would be useful for someone to behave in a certain way but foresees that it will be difficult to convince him to do so, he can deal with the problem metaphorically. For example, he can try to provoke change in some analogous aspect of his behavior. This may induce a *spontaneous* change in the problem area, for which intervention was requested. Metaphorical tasks can be assigned to individuals, to a couple, or to a whole family.

The assignment of metaphorical tasks to a whole family can produce particularly interesting results. Mr. and Mrs. Righetti have requested therapy for their two sons, Giacomo (age 4), and Bibi (age 3), because of their "abnormal" behavior. The young and apparently cooperative parents say that they feel completely unable to deal with the "destructive fury" of their two small but uncontrollable sons. Their description of the children's room makes it sound like a battle field: chairs, furniture, and toys are repeatedly destroyed by Giacomo and Bibi. The boys also have a habit of urinating in the closet. In desperation the parents have decided to eliminate almost all of the objects from the room. The children now sleep on mattresses on the floor.

The therapist immediately notices the contrast between the children's destructiveness as described by the parents and their lively but age-appropriate behavior in the therapy room. They play actively and seem to get along well with each other; they also accept their parent's explanations concerning various objects in the therapy room that draw their attention (microphone, one-way mirror, etc.). However, the therapist notices that every minimal allusion to their home life creates a sense of depression and inadequacy in both parents and sends the two children racing wildly around the room. He therefore decides not to tackle the problem directly and begins to think of analogous situations in which it might be possible to explore the parents' competence, on the one hand, and the children's acceptance of rules of behavior, on the other. He assigns the following task: the parents must go to a depart-

---

[28]This is what happens in hypnosis. A metaphorical approach is particularly effective with subjects who resist, since it is difficult to resist a directive when one is not aware of having received it. A thorough analysis of the use of metaphor in hypnosis can be found in the brilliant studies of Milton Erickson, cited by Haley (1976).

ment store and buy a miniature model bedroom with two beds, two chairs, a wardrobe, some toys, and, of course, two "children" who live in it. These toys are to be given to Giacomo and Bibi. With their parents' help, the children will learn how to take care of two "little children" and how to make them keep the furnishings of the room in order.

The family is told to spend one week in training and then to demonstrate their skill in the following session. This will give the therapist an opportunity to observe the parents' ability to teach the children how to use the toys, as well as the children's ability to accept responsibility, at least in play. The parents come to the following session carrying a large package. Giacomo and Bibi can hardly control themselves in their eagerness to open the package and begin playing. Both parents and children carry out the task with enthusiasm and are happy to show the therapist the results of their work.

The therapist congratulates them on their work but avoids making any allusions to the metaphorical significance of the task;[29] there is no need to have the family notice or understand the connection. In reality, in talking about the dollhouse and about how to teach rules of behavior to the children, the therapist is implicitly talking about how to educate Giacomo and Bibi. He is activating new forms of competence and new ways of relating between parents and children. The competence and the acceptance of rules learned in a play situation facilitate the utilization of these abilities in daily life.

Another example illustrates how metaphorical tasks can be used in therapy with couples. Therapy was requested for a series of problems; in particular, the partners were disillusioned and mutually resentful because of their sexual relationship, which they thought was a failure. In reality, the problem seemed more generalized: the couple had a redundant pattern of interacting in which *he must always win* and *she must always allow him to win*. It would have been useless to confront their sexual problem directly because although they were both dissatisfied, they invariably behaved in perfect agreement to perpetuate their *endless game*. The therapist therefore resorted to the use of metaphor to interrupt the vicious circle in which they were caught. His intention was to promote change by using an analogous situation. The therapist offered husband and wife a deck of cards and invited them to play during the session. They could play any game they wished, but they had to observe

[29]In M. Erickson's view, interpreting unconscious communications is like summarizing a play by Shakespeare in one sentence (in Haley, 1976).

one rule: the husband must always win and the wife must always lose. The couple was slightly perplexed but accepted the task. As time went by, they became intensely involved in the game and very nervous about the rigidity of the rule. At the end of the session, the therapist instructed the couple to play the game in bed before going to sleep for at least 10 minutes every night. He told them that this task was very important and he warned them about the risks involved in breaking the rules.[30]

The couple seemed visibly relieved when they arrived for the next session. They reported that they had followed the instructions for only three days; on the fourth day, the wife won, thus breaking the rule. Even more surprising was the fact that the husband had not intentionally *let* her win, and he seemed pleased by his wife's unexpected victory (even though she had broken the rule laid down by the therapist). After the fourth day, they had refused to play cards at the hour set by the therapist because the wife had started to feel strong sexual desires toward her husband—just at that hour. She had taken the initiative in sexual relations, which had proved satisfying (according to their previous statements, both her initiative in this area and the results represented new factors in their relationship).

Here, the use of a metaphorical game was effective in initiating change in the couple's rules about relating. This change enabled them to deal with their sexual problem[31] and with the dynamics of their relationship in general with greater success. The intention behind the task was to overcome the couple's resistance to change. Since this intervention reinforced their dysfunctional rules on a metaphorical level, it ultimately encouraged the formation of an alliance between the partners against the therapist. Whereas at the beginning of therapy the couple was united by their need to perpetuate their endless game, they then had to find a different way of resisting the therapist, who seemed opposed to any kind of change. To remain united, they will have to find different ways of relating. Success will depend on their own resources.

---

[30]Explaining the importance of the task and warning about the dangers of not carrying it out correctly reinforces the pragmatic effect by encouraging the couple to resist.

[31]In this brief description I have emphasized the metaphorical aspects of the task. However, this particular example also contains the characteristics of paradoxical tasks in that it prescribes to the system its own dysfunctional rules.

5

Examples of Structural Family Therapy

ACHIEVING AUTONOMY: THE CASE OF LUCIANO

Composition of the Nuclear Family

The members of the Rocci family are Attilio, the father, age 43, a salesman in a department store in Rome; Laura, the mother, age 42, occupied chiefly with running the house; and Luciano, an only child, age 16, who dropped out of school in the seventh grade and has no specific occupation at present. The identified patient is Luciano, who has been treated individually by a series of psychotherapists[1] since he was 13.

Referral and Motivation for Family Therapy

When Luciano was sent to us, he was changing from one individual therapist to another. The new therapist, however, was interested in exploring the interactional aspects of the problem and suggested taking Luciano and his family in co-therapy with me.[2]

---

[1] In this respect, the case of Luciano is similar to that of many adolescents who undergo individual psychotherapy in a discontinuous way and are passed on frequently from one therapist to another. This kind of "psychotherapeutic career" is produced by an institutional system that subordinates the continuity of the therapeutic relationship to a policy of "service," with rigid rules and hierarchies. Frequently, what is offered is a routine rather than treatment, and the resulting therapist-patient relationships tend to be superficial or even deleterious.

[2] I have chosen to report this case for several reasons: (a) It was one of my first family therapies (1970) and the first for the co-therapist, Carmine Saccu, who is now my closest collaborator. During the course of therapy, we had to deal both with our own limited

Before formulating the situation in interactional terms, I would like to summarize the information passed on to us relating to Luciano's diagnostic evaluation:

> The symptomatological picture is characterized by marked anxiety, discharged in general psychomotor instability and destructiveness; aggressiveness, acted out prevalently on objects; hypochondriacal and phobic traits (refusal to go on buses, to go out alone, etc.); and ideas of reference concerning companions and family members. On an expressive level, Luciano presents exhibitionistic behavior, verbal aggression and obscene language, alternated with ingratiating and seductive behaviors. He regards himself as the center of every event, often with paranoid compensations. He expresses anxiety with laughter, mutism, or verbal aggression. His inability to assume an active role outside of the home contrasts with his domineering behavior in the family, which his parents are powerless to deal with, despite the fact that Luciano continually requests their help. Family life is organized around Luciano's fear of being alone. This fear forces him to sleep with his mother, while the father sleeps in the living room. There is an evident contradiction between Luciano's request for autonomy and his strong dependency needs. . . .

When Saccu called Luciano in with his parents for the first time, he was struck by the boy's apparently unmotivated, arrogant—at moments almost furious—behavior. However, his behavior became more comprehensible as the therapist began to see it in relationship to the parents' behavior and to the context in which it occurred. The soup incident, cited by the parents as an example of their son's irrationality "even in little things," was particularly instructive. It helped us to see his behavior as logical and comprehensible. The incident developed in the following way:

> Luciano gets angry at his mother because the soup she has served is too salty.
> The mother disqualifies Luciano's opinion as purely symptomatic ("He is never satisfied with anything").
> The father agrees with his son emotionally (he makes visible signs of disgust), but he defends the mother, affirming that the soup is delicious.

---

experience and with a series of conflicts and contradictions between a traditional model of psychiatric intervention (which we had been taught in medical school) and an interactional model, which was at that time misunderstood and looked on with great skepticism in academic circles. (b) It seems to me a paradigmatic case for demonstrating the validity of a family approach: in fact, Luciano could achieve autonomy only if his parents were able to "let go" of him and to establish clearer generational boundaries, so that Luciano would not be drawn back into the parental subsystem. (c) We have recently reelaborated and organized the material relating to this therapy. A follow-up study four years after the conclusion of therapy helped us to evaluate the stability over time of changes obtained in therapy.

Luciano reacts with rage, overturns the soup on the table, and curses both of his parents.

Obviously, a commonplace incident of this kind can occur in any family without our attributing psychiatric implications to it. But it is less obvious that Luciano's behavior *serves the purpose* of avoiding a direct confrontation between the parents over the question of the saltiness of the soup. Although avoiding confrontation over a food problem may not necessarily create a family problem, the *avoidance of confrontation* as an habitual form of relating usually results in the creation of a scapegoat and in systemic dysfunction.

Phases of Therapy

Distinguishing the main phases of therapy will help the reader understand both the dynamics of the family and the evolution of the therapy, which consisted of weekly sessions for a period of eight months.

The Rigid Triad

In the first sessions, the family system consistently presents the structure of a rigid triad.[3] All discussion centers on Luciano, the sick boy whom the parents have brought to be cured. He sits between them while they describe his problem. During this presentation the parents appear to be united and in complete agreement with each other, and Luciano confirms their definition of the problem. On the one hand, the parents perceive all of his behavior, even the most appropriate, as symptomatic; on the other hand, Luciano tries to present himself as *the problem* of the family, and he behaves in an arrogant and domineering manner as though to confirm his parents' description of him. Description of the boy's irrational and violent behavior dominates this phase of therapy In later phases more consideration is given to Luciano's dependency and need for protection.

The entire family makes a unified effort to provide the therapists with a single definition of the problem. The parents talk about Luciano's arrogance and irrationality, which they declare themselves incapable of handling, while Luciano acts out this behavior in an ostentatious man-

[3]In a structural approach as described by Minuchin (1974), a *rigid triad* is a type of family structure with chronic problems concerning generational boundaries. The expression refers to family systems in which it is the "norm" to utilize a child in spouse conflicts.

ner both in the sessions and at home. Luciano participates in the maintenance of this rigid homeostatic equilibrium. In therapy, he claims the central position and tries to dictate to the therapists the rules of the relationship. The parents, on their part, help to maintain the equilibrium by passively accepting Luciano's behavior and by soliciting his intervention every time the therapists attempt to shift the center of attention.

The rigidity of the system becomes particularly evident when one of the therapists asks the parents to indicate another problem that they would like to resolve if Luciano's behavior were to become normal. After a long silence, interrupted only by gestures of impatience and irritation by Luciano, the parents reply in the following way:

MOTHER: Well . . . there have never been real problems between me and my husband. The problem is our son. Whether he wants to go back to school or not.

FATHER: It would concern him . . . something else about him.

MOTHER: Yes, something else about him.

After further solicitation by one of the therapists, and after another long silence, the mother continues:

MOTHER (*to the therapist*): Well, I don't know. Maybe there is a problem, but I can't seem to formulate it. Maybe there are a lot. I would need an example in order to know if I would have a problem or not. I can't tell you. Everything depends on him. I can't tell anymore . . . I don't know. . . .

After this unsuccessful attempt to sound out other possible areas of family conflict, Luciano returns to the fore. He begins to stalk about nervously and threatens to leave if we don't talk about him. He says that he is sick and wants the therapists to concentrate on him instead of wasting time on "other nonsense." Then he begins to talk about his fear of being left alone, of going on buses, and of losing weight, and about his insomnia, which makes him keep his parents awake every night. While he is describing his disturbances with dramatic emphasis, his parents remain silent, thereby communicating to the therapists their total helplessness.

The therapists are faced with the problem of gaining *access* to the system.[4] Every attempt on their part to engage the parents in a sequence of interactions that does not concern Luciano provokes a counteraction by the family system: Luciano begins to scream and insult the therapists because they are ignoring him, and whenever the parents initiate a transaction between themselves, they inevitably end up talking about their son and the gravity of the situation.

The interactional information that the therapists accumulate in this first phase of therapy indicates that the system is structurally a rigid triad, and that its preferred mechanism is the evasion of spouse conflicts, achieved by rigid utilization of Luciano. Furthermore, the parents' utilization of their son is in turn reactivated, in a circular manner, by Luciano's own behavior.[5] In this way the spouses can maintain an illusion of harmony, for they have no need to come into conflict; and Luciano, as scapegoat, protects the equilibrium of the system by continually offering himself as the family's only problem.

During the course of therapy, we discover that the evasion of spouse conflicts takes one of two alternate forms: at times, the parents *attack* their son, because he is *bad* and causes the family's problems (with his violent, hostile, and irrational behavior); at other times, the parents *protect* him, because he is *sick*, or different. In one of the first sessions, the mother observed:

> At his age kids love their parents. We all loved our parents. But when you grow up you move away from them, the kind of love you have for them is different—you know what I mean? In many ways Luciano is like a baby who still needs protection. I don't know how to explain it, but I notice him making the same gestures and doing the same things he did when he was small. . . .

Whether the parents attack Luciano because he is bad or protect him because he is sick, the result is identical: conflict between husband and wife is avoided by constantly reinforcing dysfunctional transactions in

---

[4]The problem of accessibility is of fundamental importance. Although highly dysfunctional systems present strong resistance to change, the accessibility of a system, particularly in the early phases of therapy, is evaluated in relation to the formation and growth of the therapeutic system. In other words, when the family starts therapy, it requires "emotional guarantees" before it becomes accessible and permits entrance to the therapist. The therapist, therefore, must acquire contractual power and credibility if he is to be accepted by the family members as an agent of change.

[5]"The rigid utilization of one child in spouse conflicts takes several forms. In *triangulation*, each parent demands that the child side with him against the other parent. Whenever the child sides with one, he is automatically defined as attacking the other. In this highly dysfunctional structure, the child is paralyzed; every movement he makes is defined by one parent as an attack" (Minuchin, 1974, p. 102).

the parent-child relationship. This behavior serves to maintain the only systemic balance at present acceptable to all components of the system.

Unbalancing the System

We have seen the therapists' difficulty in gathering information that does not directly concern Luciano. The prevalence of redundant behaviors (such as, "Talk only with Luciano's permission and only about him") constitutes a therapeutic *impasse* that the therapists overcome in part by assigning a task. Instead of opposing the dominant tendency of the system, the therapists support it, convinced that a paradoxical approach will interrupt the vicious circle and provide access into the family system. Accordingly, the therapists start one of the sessions by stating that at the moment it is more reassuring for everyone to talk about Luciano and that progress can be made only by concentrating all efforts on him. The therapists then assign to all three family members the task of minutely describing Luciano's behavior, since he is the source of the family's distress. This produces the desired result: Luciano is never discussed during the session, and the therapists are able to gather important information concerning some of the rules of the family system.

The mother's reaction is particularly striking. She immediately starts to speak at great length about her own childhood and that of her husband, about their loneliness, and about their marriage. Luciano does not interrupt. Even though later that week his behavior grows more turbulent and becomes the subject of discussion in the following session, it seems that the prescription has successfully begun to *destabilize* the system. The mother now communicates her ambivalent attitude toward her son, both verbally and analogically. On one hand, she is exasperated by his problems ("I feel as though his despotism is suffocating me, he keeps me tied to him by his disturbances," etc.); on the other hand, she implicitly encourages him. Ultimately, she resorts to indirectly blaming her husband for demanding too much from Luciano. She says that her husband should have more patience and consideration because of Luciano's age. In interactional terms, the mother's criticism on the one hand and reinforcement of Luciano's symptomatic behavior on the other reveal her need to maintain a stable coalition with the boy against her husband.

In another session, Luciano clearly verbalizes his mother's contradictory attitude, thus confirming our suspicion that a stable coalition exists between mother and son: "Now you make me think something else—that you did it without realizing it, because there's a part of you that doesn't want me to get well. Just like there's a part of me that wants me to stay the way I am. I'd like to get well. In fact, when I said that I had won some battles, it was the part of me that wants to get well that won. I'm up to fifty-one percent, because now the two parts balance each other. There's a part of my mother that's like me: if I get better (I'm a mama's boy, I'm attached to my mother) and I move away from her, she may not like it. But I'm very attached to my mother, and if she holds on even tighter to me, the battle is lost."

During this phase of therapy a series of clashes takes place between Luciano and his mother over questions of autonomy. However, these seem intended more to confirm the alliance between them than to deal concretely with the question of Luciano's autonomy. Nonetheless, when a family rule is uncovered and made explicit during the sessions, this in itself constitutes a modification of the system. In this case, the more explicit the alliance between Luciano and his mother becomes, the harder it will be to maintain. The exclusion of the husband, concealed behind the apparent conflict between mother and son, becomes progressively more evident, particularly with respect to the dynamics of the spouse relationship (Luciano succeeds in keeping his parents apart, in every way). During these sessions, the father seems embarrassed. When encouraged by the therapists to contribute to the discussions, he responds evasively. He seems to play the part of a second scapegoat.

The way that the wife talks about her husband, continually disqualifying the positive things she says about him, is perfectly consistent with these observations. On a verbal level, she expresses respect for him because he has always worked hard and has dedicated himself entirely to her and to their son; but her tone of voice and facial expressions communicate boredom and irritation with this insipid and monotonous man who has nothing new to offer her. In comparison to the apparent conjugal harmony presented in the initial phase of therapy, we now observe a different situation. The mother expresses her varying emotional states by venting her feelings against her attention-claiming son or, more often, against her taciturn and monotonous husband.

Now that the equilibrium of the system has been upset by modifying the mother's behavior, we expect the system to react to restore its previous homeostatic balance. In fact, Luciano tries to deny the change in his mother's attitude and attempts to restore the previous "conjugal harmony" by exaggerating his symptomatic behavior. But something has changed with respect to the family's usual method of restoring its homeostatic balance; Luciano is now forced to act out his aggressiveness on *the therapists*,[6] by whom he now feels threatened, rather than on his family, as he did formerly. This new situation demands considerable emotional self-control on the part of the therapists (Luciano threatens even physical attack—in one session he wields a steel ashtray over the head of one of the therapists). At the same time, this new situation represents an important therapeutic advance and gives the therapists access to the family system.

In systemic terms, a confrontation between the spouses is possible now that the mother-son coalition has been replaced by an open conflict between the therapists and the son. (The motives of conflict are different for each of the participants: Luciano is trying to regain his protective function at home; the therapists want to promote his independence and therefore to get him out of the house). It is clearly not easy to bring the spouses to a mutual confrontation: both husband and wife have habitually evaded their conflicts by utilizing their son, and they have never developed alternative transactional models. It is particularly significant that the father, faced with the recurring complaints of his wife, finally becomes aware of the situation and confirms the validity of our strategy of confrontation. The following are passages from the interactive sequences that marked the climax of a session:

HUSBAND: Today I am going to do the talking. Something important has happened. Yesterday, the last thing my wife said was, "We have been living together for twenty years, but there's a lot I don't know about him." Well, I think that's strange . . . I don't know, there aren't any secrets between us, she ought to know everything. Maybe she hasn't understood me. Maybe I don't express myself, I think things over in my own mind. Anyway, on Sunday afternoon, it was the time when we usually go out. We were going to go to the movies, the way we always do. I say, "Let's go to the beach instead!" That's what I said . . . I said that, and she cried. We had a talk like we never had in twenty years. We talked for two, three, four hours. It was interesting because a lot of things came out. Maybe I had been asleep, I had been pampering my-

---

[6]Provoking the patient into a direct confrontation with the therapists creates a new stage of abnormality in the family system. It is an intermediate phase that is often necessary before a solution for the real problem can be found. Although so far nothing has changed in the boy's disturbed behavior, he is now forced to act it out in relation to the therapists and continually less in relation to his parents. In structural terms, the pragmatic effect is to make the generational boundaries more flexible: Luciano, in order to confront the therapists, must abandon the territory of the spouses.

self, I thought everything was perfect. Maybe I had been so involved in my job that I never thought about it, I didn't understand, I was blind, like a horse with blinders. I don't know if you (*addressing the therapists*) are interested in hearing what was said in that talk, but there were answers to a lot of those questions that you have been asking and that you didn't get any answers to at the time. Problems? There were plenty of problems. We had never dealt with them when they came up, because I thought about them by myself, because she just accepted the situation, and later I just accepted the situation. I suffered the consequences. I let things ride. Maybe I was asleep, I don't know. Maybe I felt satisfied with what I had achieved. That's something that's still on my mind, a question. But now I'm finding answers to all of the questions that you've been asking and that I gave you silly answers to, or else I got mad at you, or maybe I didn't answer at all. There certainly were problems, loads of them, and maybe we both kept them to ourselves. We had never talked about them together. For example, there was a question you asked my wife, and Laura couldn't think of an answer. To me she said, "I didn't answer because I didn't want to offend you." (*To his wife*) You've got to answer. We are coming here for good reasons. If it is true that I was insipid, dull, that I wasn't your ideal, say so! You don't offend me. You said, "You have some good qualities, but perhaps I expected something more." Admit it, admit that that's the truth!

WIFE (*to the therapists*): When you asked me what feelings I have toward my husband, I said, "Less than for my son." But I would have preferred not to answer that question, because if I had been sincere, I would have had to say none, none at all.

HUSBAND: It's like an assembly line.

WIFE (*to her husband*): I have always felt these things. It's just that . . . I tried to tell you, but you always felt hurt and for two or three days wouldn't even look at me. So I gave up.

HUSBAND: You should have insisted . . . but it's not that I wasn't listening. Maybe I didn't understand, maybe I didn't see things. You should have insisted, you should have insisted.

In the previous sessions, Attilio had been reticent and had allowed himself to be dominated. Now, in venting his feelings, his tone of voice is vibrant and decisive. He holds the central position for the entire ses-

sion and counters every effort by Luciano to interfere. During the subsequent course of therapy, he at times reverts to his habitual behavior as
a silent, marginal father and husband, but his new awareness represents
a first step toward a redefinition of roles and functions in the family.

The father's revelations and the direct interaction between the
spouses pose a further threat to the equilibrium of the system. Luciano,
now faced with the problems of his parents, attempts to win back his
role as catalyzer of family tensions. He exaggerates his symptoms—his
fear of abandonment and his phobias as well as his violent reactions to
his parents—and in the sessions, every time the discussion tends to
center on the parents, he calls attention to himself by demonstrating
how "sick" he is. This can be clearly observed in the following exchange
between the mother and Luciano.

MOTHER (*to the therapists*): Something is changing, but it's something he
doesn't like. He is furious at you, because you are the ones who are
responsible for it, you see? Otherwise, I wouldn't be able to explain the
things he has been saying against you, these past days at home. It's a
sign that you have stirred up something inside of him that he doesn't
want to let out.

LUCIANO (*during this session he expresses his fear of changing very clearly*): I
want to cooperate with you, but I see you as enemies. That is, I don't
really think that. . . . You're trying to help me, aren't you? But I try to go
against you and not let myself get cured. I've thought about these
things, only I don't want to admit them to myself, you know what I
mean? That's the whole problem. If I admit it to myself, I feel nervous.
So I blow up at something else.

Clarifying Generational Boundaries

Although Luciano continues to behave as the protagonist in the sessions, monopolizing everyone's attention, the system's resistance to
change seems less rigid than in the initial phase of therapy. This di-
minished rigidity is undoubtedly due to the fact that the parents have
gained greater security and are now able to deal concretely with the
problems between them, both in the sessions and at home. Although
Luciano's symptoms seem to have "grown" in this period, they have
lost their power to evoke an emotional response from the parents and,
more importantly, they seem to have changed their objective. Instead of

being directed toward the family, they are now directed toward the outer world, temporarily represented by the therapeutic team. The therapists now formulate a strategy to encourage Luciano to seek greater autonomy so that generational boundaries can be more clearly delineated. Once the triad becomes less rigid—that is, once spouse confrontation is no longer felt to be threatening and intolerable to everyone—and once Luciano no longer needs to act as catalyzer of family tensions and can give up his protective role, then a redefinition of the relationships between the spouses and the son will finally be possible.

The therapists decide to encourage this process by assigning a *task intended to create a new scapegoat*. A strategy is designed that will temporarily transfer Luciano's *disturbances* to his father. We decide to utilize the father's sphere of activity outside of the family.

The father has never missed a day's work in 20 years from his job as a salesman in a large department store. His job is perhaps the only area in his life that provides him with real satisfaction and in which his competence is recognized by everyone, including his wife and son. One of the therapists, in an individual session with him, requests his help in stimulating Luciano to take on some kind of responsibility outside of the home. The therapist assigns the following task: the father must take a 15-day leave from work; at home, he is to behave as though he were unusually depressed and neglectful, and he must refuse to communicate in any way with his wife and son.

In presenting the task, the therapist tells him that it will probably not be difficult to feel depressed; 15 days at home will give him an opportunity to discover important and upsetting aspects of family roles and functions. This therapeutic move is bound to provoke a strong reaction, particularly in Luciano. In fact, at the next session, Luciano attacks the therapists, whom he holds responsible for his father's illness, and he announces his decision to become the family's representative outside the home ("If he is in this state, then I will have to take over").

The task is clearly a provocation to Luciano, and it sets in motion—in a way that is unusual but decidedly effective—an evolution toward greater autonomy in Luciano and a complete revision of family roles. Luciano does not come to the sessions for a certain period of time, but he sends messages to the therapists through his parents. These messages are reassuring about himself; they implicitly confirm the validity of our strategy and indicate that the time is ripe for dealing with spouse problems, without Luciano's mediation. In fact, the parents, no longer "blocked" by Luciano's symptoms, begin to act out their disagreements and their conflicts through more direct and authentic interactions and to explore the possibilities for creating a new kind of relationship. Luciano's greater autonomy outside of the family corresponds to a rediscovery of common interests on the part of the spouses, who are now seeking a different and more genuine marital relationship. For the first time in 16 years they are experiencing being together without Luciano.

Negotiating Reciprocal Autonomy

The therapy now seems to be moving toward its main objective—the separation of the generational units in the family. This process of differentiation, further promoted by Luciano's absence from several sessions, is subsequently reinforced by the therapists by holding separate sessions with Luciano.

In the individual sessions with Luciano the therapists abandon their provocative approach. Luciano is now willing to establish a different kind of relationship, which will help him to consolidate his progress toward emancipation. Discussion focuses on his job, his companions, and his girl friend, and in general, on his way of dealing with reality. Despite his frequent swings from a grandiose evaluation of himself to doubts about his ability to get along adequately with his peers, he is now dealing with his own problems of personal growth, and he is gradually giving up his role as family scapegoat.

The spouses have overcome their fear of intimacy which had led to the confusion of generational roles and functions. They are now in a position to deal with a problem that only a few months earlier seemed insoluble—restructuring the family in a way that restores to Luciano his position as son and to the couple their own marital territory.

Previously all efforts to deal with the problem of sleeping arrangements had failed, because they had been determined more by the therapists' anxiety than by correct therapeutic *timing*.

Four Years Later

Therapy terminated after approximately eight months. The family kept in contact with the therapists through periodic meetings (about one a year), in which the therapists received information about the general state of the family and were able to observe the permanence of the changes initiated during therapy. In these meetings, each therapist played the part of a family friend interested in hearing about the phases of development of the family group. Luciano spoke openly about his Sardinian girl friend and about the customs of the island, while the parents proudly talked about their vacations in the mountains.

I saw the family again four years after the conclusion of therapy. The family accepted my invitation willingly, and during our encounter, the family members remembered the fundamental phases of therapy very clearly. Recalling the time when Luciano monopolized all attention with his parents' complicity, I was struck by the family's new way of being together, based on reciprocal respect. When I asked them about the most significant events of the last four years, the parents spoke about themselves and about their relationship, which they considered more mature and authentic. The wife looked younger and was eager to tell that she felt freer and more autonomous. The husband, too, spoke about their relationship. He described it as "having found each other again" after a long time, and he seemed resolute and self-confident. They treated Luciano as an adult and seemed to find pleasure in his company.

Luciano sat at a distance from his parents and spoke at length about the changes that had occurred. He behaved like a young adult capable of dealing with the problems of his age in an autonomous way, without need for exhibitionism or dependency. He described the significant events of the period while his parents listened attentively. He talked about his work in a clothing store, interrupted only for his term of military service. He spoke about his life in the army, which had ended only a few days previously. He had been very worried at the beginning, fearing that military life would be too much for him emotionally. However, he had successfully adapted to a reality that was neither easy nor pleasant and had gotten through it without negative repercussions. In fact, this first experience away from home had enabled him to judge his capacities more realistically. He had made many friends, which his parents mentioned with satisfaction. Some of these friends, who had finished their military service at the same time, had invited him to spend his summer vacation in Sardinia, together with his girl friend, Paola. After the summer, he was going to work in the postal service, where he had been offered a permanent job. The idea of a permanent job—like the necessity of assuming personal responsibility in general—undoubtedly caused him some anxiety. But his worries were those of any adolescent, and they were no longer considered exceptional.

The emotional atmosphere in the family had changed to one of profound reciprocal respect. The mother explained that their new family philosophy came from the maternal grandmother ("everyone for himself"). The identification of areas of personal autonomy has permitted the family to develop new ways of relating based on greater self-knowledge and on reciprocal trust. The family was now a unit composed of distinct and differentiated parts. The system no longer depended on the deviation of spouse conflicts and the maintenance of a scapegoat. Family members could confront each other more freely at all levels, and above all, there had been a *true emancipation* of all the adults, including Luciano.

A FAMILY WITH AN ENCOPRETIC CHILD[7]

The T. family was referred by a pediatrician at the Children's Hospital in Philadelphia, where the mother had gone for help because Andy, during the previous year, had been "crapping in his pants" several times a day, even at school. After a series of laboratory tests was carried out at the hospital, all yielding negative results, the pediatrician advised brief family therapy at the Philadelphia Child Guidance Clinic.[8]

This black family consisted of the mother, Carolyn, who was 36, and four children: Sandra, 13; Andy, the identified patient, 12; Charlene, 7; and Robert, 6. The parents had been separated for several years. The father, Howard, was a cab driver who was living with another woman on the outskirts of the city and kept up only sporadic contact with the children. Carolyn and the children lived in an extremely poor area. Despite a difficult economic situation, Carolyn did her best to provide for the basic needs of her children and seemed to take pride in her role as a mother. She had refused to accept assistance from welfare; she managed to maintain the family with dignity, enabling all of her children to attend school, with the wages from her job as a cleaning woman for an airline company. The children had learned to be self-sufficient and assumed many responsibilities when their mother was at work.

[7]The material in this section is from my article, "A Structural Approach to a Family with an Encopretic Child," which appeared in the *Journal of Marriage and Family Counseling,* 1978, pp. 25-29, and is reprinted with the permission of the publisher.
[8]I treated the T. family for a period of four months at the Philadelphia Child Guidance Clinic, under the supervision of Jay Haley, to whom I express my deep appreciation.

Therapeutic Stages

Focusing on the Presenting Problem to Gain Access to the Family System

In the first sessions, the problem of encopresis was examined in detail in order to understand what it represented for his mother, for Andy, and for his older sister Sandra, and to what extent each one was willing to cooperate to overcome this difficulty. They all agreed in evaluating the encopretic behavior as inadequate and troublesome, and they saw no explanation for it. Carolyn was burdened with the extra work of washing her son's underwear every day, but she was above all worried that the disturbance could be of a mental nature. (This fear appeared more comprehensible when later, in an individual session, the mother talked about her husband's hospitalization in a psychiatric facility, which had occurred when they were still living together.) For Sandra, Andy's disturbance offered an opportunity to act as a deputy mother, responsible for running the house when their mother was absent. Andy seemed upset by his own apparently incomprehensible behavior and felt ashamed of it because it was not suitable to his age.

After gathering basic relational information on the problem, the therapeutic approach was initially directed toward establishing a cordial and cheerful context in which mother and children were able to have play periods. Carolyn was usually so busy with her job and the responsibilities of running the family that she was never able to find time to relax or to play with her children. During one of the sessions, the children were asked to organize a game that their mother also enjoyed. The game not only stimulated play between mother and children (the children later reported that they had repeated the game at home); it also helped the therapist to join the family and to explore the relationships among the children.[9] In fact, two groups had existed in the children's subsystem: one formed by the older ones, Andy and Sandra, and another formed by the younger ones, Charlene and Robert. The appearance of the encopretic behavior had brought confusion into the chil-

---

[9]The capacity to play together, to share common interests, and to offer each other mutual support against their parents is an indication of the degree of rigidity in the problem child's role as scapegoat. Ultimately, children's capacities in this sense are inversely proportional to the degree of tension and stress expressed by the family system.

dren's hierarchy, relegating Andy to the younger, more dependent group, and moving Sandra into the parental subsystem.

With these considerations in mind, I tried from the beginning to enter into an alliance with Andy, utilizing my language difficulties in this effort.[10] For example, I asked Andy to explain some black slang expressions that were incomprehensible to me. The task was willingly accepted by the boy, who was proud of his role as a language consultant.

Two restructuring operations were applied in this first phase: a redistribution of responsibilities in the children's subsystem and the creation of an alliance between Andy and the therapist. One session was used to verify what duties Sandra and Andy had at home. Sandra had greater responsibilities than Andy, who in turn was resentful of this situation. When asked what each one thought about this unequal distribution of tasks, they both said that they would prefer greater equality. Carolyn also favored an equal distribution of chores.

During one of the sessions, Andy and Sandra were requested to renegotiate their responsibilities, especially concerning the care of Charlene and Robert during their mother's absence. Carolyn was asked to act as an impartial mediator. The resulting redistribution of duties was discussed in the following sessions. This restructuring operation gave rapid results: Carolyn offered her full cooperation because she felt she was receiving real help for her children, although such help was not yet directed toward the problem for which she had originally asked assistance. By supporting the agreed-upon redistribution of tasks, Carolyn gave impetus to Andy's newfound competency. Furthermore, the restructuring reduced the parental role played by Sandra and enabled her to experience her adolescence more fully.

At this point in the therapy, I formed an exclusive alliance with Andy. During the course of the following sessions I divided the family. In order to have an opportunity to hold brief conversations with Andy alone, I offered to help him with his encopresis, on condition that it remain a secret between him and me. Andy brightened up and was very pleased by the offer.

I then assigned him the task of keeping a personal diary in which he

---

[10]The therapeutic utility of expressing oneself in a limited way in a foreign language is amazing. It permits the therapist to pretend that he has not understood whenever he wants to draw attention to an important sequence or interaction. It also encourages the spontaneous collaboration of the family, which is always ready to help a therapist in difficulty.

was to note each day when and where he soiled his pants. He was asked to bring the diary with him to our following meetings so that we could analyze it together in order to have a complete view of the problem.

The technique described above was utilized to modify the *relational meaning of the symptom*, which Andy was now acting out for the therapist, rather than for his family. His encopresis, which was initially a means of communication within the family, became the central content of the growing relationship between the boy and the therapist, which fulfilled Andy's need for an area in which to express his own personality outside the family context, in accordance with the needs of his preadolescent phase of development. In a certain sense, this represented a transition from the original situation of "abnormality," which had caused the request for a therapeutic intervention, to a temporary, artificial situation encouraged by the therapist in order to promote change by unbalancing the family system and thereby creating new alternatives. At the same time, talking about the symptom as if it were a work project, with schedules and deadlines, ultimately rendered it ridiculous and untenable and gradually made it possible for Andy to explore other concerns.

This *strategy of provocation* in the treatment of a symptom has often proved to be a determining factor in overcoming even serious disturbances in young children and adolescents. In this kind of approach the therapist directly challenges the disturbed behavior and at the same time makes a constant effort to enhance the person by encouraging and reinforcing the positive aspects of his behavior. In Andy's case the therapeutic alliance, which was initially based on the presenting problem, gradually expanded to include a broader range of adolescent problems, once the function of the symptom in the family system had been understood.

From Encopresis to the Problem of the Family

The improvement in Andy's symptom must be considered from a systemic perspective. The therapist's alliance with Andy and the provocative strategy employed represent only part of a broader plan, which had first required a redefinition of boundaries and responsibilities at the level of the sibling subsystem, and which then had to be completed by a restructuring at the level of the parents. This second task was complicated by the fact that the parents were separated, so that at this point, the therapy had to focus on the mother in order to obtain a clearer understanding of the parents' situation. Individual sessions were held with Carolyn, and the following are some of the important elements that emerged. First, there was an implicit confirmation of an improvement in Andy, as Carolyn appeared visibly relieved and no longer even mentioned the problem of her son's encopresis. Instead she seemed to be seeking help for herself, which was immediately offered. Some of her own conflicts came to light: in particular a relationship with a man, which she had maintained for some time and which created in her a deep sense of guilt toward the children. On the one hand, she felt a need for affection and personal support; on the other, she feared that the children would blame her for not dedicating all of her energy to their upbringing.

The problem of her husband also came into discussion; she had felt no attachment to him for years, but she realized that the children, particularly Andy, suffered from his absence. When the children questioned her about their father, she always answered evasively; for example, when they asked about his psychiatric hospitalization, Carolyn often used this as a pretext to justify his absence from home. I asked Carolyn whether she thought that the children were old enough to discuss their father more fully and directly. Carolyn accepted this possibility and she and the children discussed the father openly in the following session. In this way the father's hospitalization was put in a different perspective, and both Carolyn and the children seemed interested in and respectful of each other's feelings. The discussion undoubtedly put an emotional strain on Carolyn but ultimately had a liberating effect on her feelings of guilt.

Andy participated in this session with particular interest, implicitly demonstrating his desire to reestablish contact with his father. Sandra was very close to her mother and understood her feelings. Robert and Charlene were very happy when they realized that their father was no longer in the hospital, but then they could not understand why he did not come to visit them.

At this point the relational significance of Andy's encopresis was evident, as was its function as an *alarm signal* indicating a deeply troubled situation that had disturbed the family on many levels for a long time but that had never been dealt with directly. The improvement of the symptom, although it had not yet entirely disappeared, also seemed to indicate that the therapeutic approach was correct, but that there was still work to be done. The problem was no longer Andy's encopresis, but rather the need to find a new model of family relationships that would be better suited to the requirements of all members.

The need for familial restructuring seemed to gain explicit confirmation during a session in which Andy appeared more mature and eager to find a different role for himself within the family. I discussed with the mother the possibilities of seeking a new form of relationship between Howard and the children, without committing her to any renewed involvement with her former husband. A positive relationship between father and children would make it easier for Carolyn to accept her own relationship with another man without feeling guilty. Carolyn gave her consent, although she feared that Howard would not be willing to see the children, as he had not been in the past, and that a refusal on his part might have a negative effect on the children.

I felt that the most suitable person to contact Howard was Andy, so I met him in the coffee shop of the Child Guidance Clinic and asked him whether he thought he could locate his father and invite him to a session together with the children. Andy was surprised by the proposal and confided proudly that he knew the address of the cab depot where his father worked. Howard accepted Andy's invitation, and the meeting took place the following week. I described to him in a general way how the therapy had been proceeding, and I explained the reasons for which we had invited him.

Howard said that he had come willingly; he seemed very affectionate with the children, although clearly embarrassed about his long absence. He had last seen the children about a year ago, before Andy had evidenced any disturbance. I told him that the children had discussed some of their expectations toward him and that they wanted to express these directly to him, if he agreed. Howard offered to cooperate and encouraged the children to present their requests. Several sessions were dedicated to negotiating new ways of getting together in order to reinforce the affective bonds between them. During these sessions I often left them alone to emphasize, by my absence, that they were to reach an agreement with each other, not with me. The last session was devoted exclusively to Carolyn and Howard. Carolyn had appreciated her husband's participation in the sessions, although she was skeptical about the duration of his commitment. While I appreciated her doubts, I also supported her husband, who had never before assumed his responsibilities in such a clear way.

I saw the family again in a follow-up session about two years after the end of treatment. Andy was going every week to see his father on duty at the cab depot. Carolyn had found another less tiring and better-paid job and was continuing her extramarital relationship, which no longer caused her to feel guilty toward her children. The father had maintained his agreement with the children and was very happy about the periodic visits of Andy, whom he was teaching to repair cars. Sandra had matured and held a part-time job in a record store. Charlene and Robert were getting along well, with no serious problems. The family came willingly to this meeting and indicated that the changes that had matured during and after therapy continued to be effective. I personally learned much from my experience with the T. family: above all, that racial and national differences do not create an obstacle as long as a loyal and cooperative context, based on mutual acceptance, can be established.

Bibliography

Ackerman, N. W. Child participation in family therapy. *Family Process*, 1970, 9, 403-410.

Alger, J. Audio-visual techniques in family therapy. In D. Block (Ed.), *Techniques of family psychotherapy*. New York: Grune & Stratton, 1973.

Andolfi, M. Paradox in psychotherapy. *American Journal of Psychoanalysis, 34*, 1974, 221-228.

Andolfi, M. I fattori sociologici della farmacodipendenza dei giovani. *Difesa Sociale, 3*, 1975, 3-32.

Andolfi, M. A structural approach to a family with an encopretic child. *Journal of Marriage and Family Counseling*, 1978, 4, 25-29.

Andolfi, M. Redefinition in family therapy. *American Journal of Family Therapy*, Spring, 1979.

Andolfi, M., & Menghi, P. La prescrizione in terapia familiare: Parte prima. *Archivio di Psicologia, Neurologia e Psichiatria, 4*, 1976, 434-456. (a)

Andolfi, M., & Menghi, P. La terapia con la famiglia. *Neuropsichiatria Infantile, 180,* 1976, 487-498. (b)

Andolfi, M., & Menghi, P. La prescrizione in terapia familiare: Parte seconda. *Archivio di Psicologia, Neurologia e Psichiatria, 1*, 1977, 57-76.

Andolfi, M., Stein, D., & Skinner, J. A system approach to the child, school, family and community in an urban area. *American Journal of Community Psychology*, Dec. 1976.

Anzilotti, J., & Giacometti, K. Presentation to the Italian translation of C. Whitaker, Psychotherapy of the absurd. *Terapia Familiare, 1*, 1977, 111-113.

Aponte, H. J. Psychotherapy for the poor: An eco-structural approach to treatment. *Delaware Medical Journal*, March 1974.

Aponte, H. J. The family-school interview: An eco-structural approach. *Family Process, 15,* 1976, 303-212.

Auerswald, E. H. Interdisciplinary vs. ecological approach. *Family Process, 7,* 1968, 202-215.

Auerswald, E. H. Families, change and the ecological perspective. In A. Ferber, M. Mendelsohn, & A. Napier (Eds.), *The book of family therapy*. New York: Science House, 1972.

Basaglia, F. *L'istituzione negata*. Torino: Einaudi, 1968.

Barten, H. H., & Barten, S. S. *Children and their parents in brief therapy*. New York: Behavioral Publications, 1973.

Bateson, G. *Steps to an ecology of mind*. New York: Ballantine Books, 1972.

Bateson, G., Jackson, D. D., Haley, J., & Weakland, J. Toward a theory of schizophrenia. *Behavioral Science*, *1*, 1956, 251-264.

Bernstein, B. Language and social class. *British Journal of Sociology*, *11*, 1960, 271-276.

Bertalanffy, L. *General system theory*. New York: George Braziller, 1969.

Boszormenyi-Nagi, I., & Framo, J. (Eds.). *Intensive family therapy*. New York: Harper & Row, 1965.

Bowen, M. The use of family theory in clinical practice. *Comprehensive Psychiatry*, *9*, 1966.

Cancrini, L. *Bambini "diversi" a scuola*. Torino: Boringhieri, 1974.

Cancrini, L. Introduction to the Italian edition of J. Haley, *Strategies of psychotherapy*, [*Le strategie della psicoterapia*], Firenze: Sansoni, 1974.

Cancrini, L., Andolfi, M., Angrisani, P., Cancrini, G., Coletti, M., Fioravanti, G., Malagoli Togliatti, M., & Marzot, A., Analisi del modello interattivo ed esperienze di terapia familiare. *L'Ospedale Psichiatrico*, 1972.

Cancrini, L., & Malagodi Togliatti, M. *Psichiatria e rapporti sociali*. Roma: Editori Riuniti, 1976.

Duhl, F. J., Kantor, D., & Duhl, B. S. Learning, space and action in family therapy: A primer of sculpture. In D. Block (Ed.), *Techniques of family psychotherapy*. New York: Grune & Stratton, 1973.

Dunlop, K. A revision of the fundamental law of habit formation. *Science*, *67*, 1928, 360-362.

Eagle, C. J., & Ray, D. The problem-solving group: A quadripartite system approach to school behavior problems. Paper presented at the 49th annual meeting of the American Orthopsychiatric Association, April 1972.

Ekman, P., Sorenson, R., & Friesen, W. V. Pan-cultural elements in facial displays of emotion. *Science*, *164*, 1969.

Ferber, A., Mendelsohn, M., & Napier, A. (Eds.). *The book of family therapy*. New York: Science House, 1972.

Frankl, V. E. *The doctor and the soul*. New York: Knopf, 1957.

Glick, D., & Haley, J. *Family therapy and research*. An annotated bibliography of articles and books published 1950-1970. New York: Grune & Stratton, 1971.

Goffman, E. *Behavior in public places*. Glencoe, Ill.: Free Press, 1963.

Guerin, J. P. (Ed.). *Family therapy: Theory and practice*. New York: Gardner Press, 1976.

Haley, J. Paradoxes in play, fantasy and psychotherapy. *Psychiatric Research Reports*, *2*, 1955, 52-58.

Haley, J. *Strategies of psychotherapy*. New York: Grune & Stratton, 1963.

Haley, J. *Changing families*. New York: Grune & Stratton, 1971.

Haley, J. *Uncommon Therapy*. New York: Norton, 1973.

Haley, J. Why a mental health clinic should avoid family therapy. *Journal of Marriage and Family Counseling*, Jan. 1975.

Haley, J. *Problem-solving therapy*. San Francisco: Jossey-Bass, 1976.

Haley, J., & Hoffman, L. *Techniques of family therapy*. New York: Basic Books, 1967.

Hall, E. T. *The hidden dimension*. Garden City, N.Y.: Doubleday, 1966.

Hochmann, J. *Pour une psychiatrie communautaire*. Paris: Editions du Seuil, 1971.

Hoffman, L. Deviation-amplifying process in natural groups. In J. Haley (Ed.), *Changing families*. New York: Grune & Stratton, 1971.

Hollingshead, A., & Redlich, F. *Social class and mental illness*. New York: Wiley, 1958.

Horney, K. *The neurotic personality of our time*. New York: Norton, 1964.

Jackson, D. D. A suggestion for the technical handling of paranoid patients. *Psychiatry*, *25*, 1963, 306-307.

Jervis, G. *Manuale critico di psichiatria*. Milano: Feltrinelli, 1975.

Kaffman, M. Short-term family therapy. *Family Process*, *2*, 1963, 216-234.

Laing, R. *The politics of the family*. Toronto: CBC Publications, 1969.

Laing, R., & Esterson, A. *Sanity, madness and the family.* London: Tavistock Publications, 1964.

Laquer, H. P. Multiple family therapy and general systems theory. In N. Ackerman (Ed.), *Family therapy in transition.* Boston: Little Brown, 1970.

Lévi-Strauss, C. *Razza e storia e altri studi di antropologia.* Torino: Einaudi, 1967.

Lewis, O. *La vida.* New York: Vintage Books, 1968.

Menghi, P. Terapia familiare: Valutazioni critiche di una metodologia di intervento. *La Rivista di Servizio Sociale, 2,* 1976, 36-42.

Minuchin, S. The use of an ecological framework in the treatment of a child. In J. Anthony & C. Koupernik (Eds.), *The child in his family.* New York: Wiley & Sons, 1970.

Minuchin, S. *Families and family therapy.* Cambridge: Harvard University Press, 1974.

Minuchin, S., Montalvo, B., Guerney, B. J. R., Rosman, B., & Shumer, F. *Families of the slums.* New York: Basic Books, 1967.

Montagu, A. *Touching.* New York: Harper & Row, 1972.

Montalvo, B. Aspects of live supervision. *Family Process, 12,* 1973, 343-360.

Montalvo, B., & Haley, J. In defense of child therapy. *Family Process, 12,* 1973, 227-244.

Nicoló, A. M. Tecniche di azione in terapia familiare: La scultura. *Neuropsichiatria Infantile, 190,* 1977, 421-441.

Papp, P. Sculpting and commentary, *The Family, 1,* 1973, 44-47.

Papp, P., Silverstein, O., & Carter, E. Family sculpting in preventive work with well families. *Family Process, 12,* 1973, 197-212.

Parsons, T., & Bales, R. *Family, socialization and interaction process.* Glencoe, Ill.: Free Press, 1955.

Rosen, J. *Direct analysis.* New York: Grune & Stratton, 1953.

Sager, C., & Singer Kaplan, H. *Progress in group and family therapy.* New York: Brunner-Mazel, 1972.

Scheflen, A. *Body language and the social order.* Englewood Cliffs, N.J.: Prentice-Hall, 1972.

Selvini Palazzoli, M , Contesto e metacontesto nella psicoterapia della famiglia. *Archivio di Psicologia Neurologia y Psichiatria, 3,* 1970, 203-211.

Selvini Palazzoli, M., Boscolo, L., Cecchin, G., & Prata, G. *Paradox and counterparadox.* New York: Aronson, 1978.

Selvini Palazzoli, M. *et al. Il mago smagato,* Milano: Feltrinelli, 1976.

Skolnick, A., & Skolnick, J. *The family in transition.* Boston: Little Brown, 1971.

Sluzki, C. E. The coalitionary process in initiating family therapy. *Family Process, 14,* 1975, 67-78.

Sluzki, C. E., & Ranson, D. C. (Eds.). *Double bind: The foundation of the communicational approach to the family.* New York: Grune & Stratton, 1976.

Sluzki, C. E., & Verón, E. The double bind as a universal pathogenic situation. *Family Process, 10,* 1971, 397-417.

Speck, R., & Attneave, C. *Family networks.* New York: Pantheon Books, 1973.

Speer, D. C. Family systems: Morphostasis or morphogenesis, or, is homeostasis enough? *Family Process, 3,* 1970, 259-278.

Vogel, E. F., & Bell, N. *A modern introduction to the family.* New York: Free Press, 1960.

Walrond-Skinner, S. *Family therapy.* London: Routledge & Kegan Paul, 1976.

Watzlawick, P., Weakland, J. H. & Fisch, R. *Change.* New York: Norton, 1974. Norton, 1967.

Watzlawick, P., Weakland, J. H. & Fisch, R. *Change.* New York; Norton, 1974.

Weakland, J., Fisch, R., Watzlawick, P., & Bodin, A. Brief therapy: focused problem resolution. *Family Process, 13,* 1974, 141-168.

Whitaker, C. Psychotherapy of the absurd; with a special emphasis on the psychotherapy of aggression. *Family Process, 14,* 1975, 1-16.

Wittgenstein, L. *Remarks on the foundations of mathematics.* Oxford: Basil Blackwell, 1956.

Wynne, L., Ryckoff, M., Day, J., & Hirsch, S. Pseudo-mutuality in the family relations of schizophrenics. *Psychiatry, 21,* 1958, 205-220.

Zuk, G., & Boszormenyi-Nagy, I. *Family therapy and disturbed families.* Palo Alto, Ca.: Science and Behavior Books, 1969.

Index

167